CASH MANAGEMENT AND THE PAYMENTS SYSTEM: Ground Rules, Costs, and Risks

The Globecon Group
Henry A. Davis
Director, Consulting Services

A Publication of
Financial Executives Research Foundation

Cash Management and the Payments System:
Ground Rules, Costs, and Risks

Financial Executives Research Foundation
10 Madison Avenue, P.O. Box 1938
Morristown, New Jersey 07960

International Standard Book Number 0-910586-62-4
Library of Congress Catalog Card Number 86-82305
Printed in the United States of America

First Printing

Book Design by Malcolm Grear Designers

Financial Executives Research Foundation is the research affiliate of Financial Executives Institute. The Foundation's basic purpose is to conduct fundamental research and publish authoritative material in the field of business management, with particular emphasis on the principles and practices of financial management and its evolving role in the management of business.

Project Advisory Committee

Donald Cannon
Treasurer
Shell Oil Co.

Arden B. Engebretsen
CFO, Corporate Vice President, & Treasurer
Hercules Incorporated

R. Max Gould
Senior Vice President & Division Head
Citibank

Roland L. Laing
Director of Research
Financial Executives Research Foundation

Wilmer Leinbach
Executive Vice President & CFO
First Fidelity Bank, Newark

Frederick H. Ober
Senior Research Associate
Financial Executives Research Foundation

James L. Weaver (Chairman)
Vice President & Treasurer
General Mills, Inc.

Marilyn Buckingham
Publications Associate
Financial Executives Research Foundation

Acknowledgments

The following individuals contributed to the design of the questionnaire and helped in reviewing all stages of the project: Patricia E. Dowden, Vice President, Philadelphia National Bank; Mel Herman, Managing Director, Globecon Group; David B. Humphrey, Vice President & Payments System Adviser, Federal Reserve Bank of Richmond; Gerald Kramer, Managing Director, Globecon Group; Frederick C. Militello, Jr., Managing Director, Globecon Group; Kenneth L. Parkinson, President, Treasury Communications & Editor, *Journal of Cash Management;* and Susan Clark Shellington, Assistant Director-Treasury Financial Services, Bell Atlantic & Government Relations Committee Chair, National Corporate Cash Management Assoc. Ms. Dowden coordinated this project with the work of Roland K. Bullard, Vice Chairman, Philadelphia National Bank and Chairman of the Large Dollar Payments System Advisory Group. Ms. Shellington, in conjunction with Raymond P. Ruzek, Executive Director, National Corporate Cash Management Assoc., arranged for our findings to be shared with those of the NCCMA in their recent survey.

Special thanks go to the 48 financial executives, financial analysts, commercial bankers, and others from 40 institutions, a number of whom are quoted in the book, who provided invaluable information and insights in the form of both interviews and written material. Their names are listed in the appendix.

Contents

Introduction

In early 1986, the Financial Executives Research Foundation commissioned the Globecon Group, a New York-based financial consulting firm, to examine current trends in corporate cash management and changes in the nation's payments system. Two events were of particular interest when planning for the study began, the E. F. Hutton incident and the forthcoming voluntary daylight overdraft limits for banks. At that time, corporate financial officers began to ask their bankers, lawyers, and auditors which cash management practices were legal and ethical and which were not. Financial officers also asked their banks how daylight overdraft caps would affect their own money transfers. They wondered whether a gridlock in the nation's high-volume and fast-moving money transfer system could occur at some point during the working day when several large banks simultaneously reached their daylight overdraft limits.

Using the Hutton incident and the daylight overdraft limits as starting points, we undertook a study of the trends underlying these events. Our objective was to identify changes in ground rules and priorities as corporate cash management reached a stage of maturity, and the U.S. payments system evoled as a result of increased volume, automation, and risk.

Information for the study has come from detailed questionnaires sent to corporations and banks; from interviews with corporations, banks, consultants, and government officials; numerous books and articles, and surveys conducted by the National Corporate Cash Management Association (NCCMA) and Greenwich Research Associates. Corporate questionnaires were sent to Financial Executives Institute members, who either answered them personally or sent them to individuals within their companies who were more directly concerned with cash management. Bank questionnaires were sent to the heads of cash management functions, who tended to be very familiar with the daylight overdraft issue or in close touch with those who were. In all, 197 questionnaires were returned from corporations and 53 were received from banks.

We did not want the study to focus exclusively on the very large corporation, but we recognized that the need, opportunity, and complexity of cash management become greater as the corporation becomes larger. About 60% of our respondents have sales over $1 billion, 30% had sales from $100 million to $1 billion; and 10% had sales less than $100 million.

Corporate responses were received from companies of various sizes and industries in all geographic regions in the United States. Twenty-five percent are manufacturers of consumer goods; 20% are manufacturers of capital, transportation, high technology, and other heavy industrial products. Fifteen percent are in processing industries, such as chemicals, petroleum, metals, textiles, paper, and rubber, and 15% are in transportation. Other respondents are in retailing, broadcasting and publishing, utilities, hotels and restaurants, insurance and other financial services. Tabulations of the questionnaires were broken down by size and industry to identify whether cash management techniques, problems, or perceptions varied among those categories.

Responses were returned by 53 of the top 300 U.S. banks in deposit size, as ranked by the *American Banker*. Seven of the top 20 banks responded. We received 11 responses from banks ranked 21 to 50, and 9 from banks ranked 51 to 100.

Replies to the bank and corporate questionnaires are summarized and analyzed in the text. Copies of selected questions and answers are in Appendices B and C.

1 Cash Management and the Payments System: A Product of the U.S. Banking Structure

The art of cash management has been one of the most important developments in corporate finance since World War II. The cost of maintaining cash has become too high for any major corporation to ignore the practice. A host of corporate techniques and bank products has been developed to cope with the peculiarities of the mail system, the payments system, and the underlying banking structure in the United States. Cash management and the payments system have been evolving in tandem with changes in technology and the financial markets. This study explores some recent trends and their implications for cash management and the payments system in the near future. A few definitions and some historical background will help the reader understand these trends.

What is Cash Management?

Cash management encompasses a number of functions within the corporate treasury, including:

1. *Collecting* cash from customers.
2. *Concentrating* cash where it can be most efficiently deployed.
3. *Disbursing* cash to vendors.

4. *Investing* surplus cash.
5. *Borrowing* to meet short-term cash deficiencies.
6. *Managing bank relations.*
7. *Forecasting* and related techniques to predict future funds flows.
8. *Managing "internal float" and other treasury operations* that have some impact on the speed with which (a) orders are taken from the customer, (b) payment terms are defined, (c) invoices are prepared and sent, and (d) cash is collected. That sequence is sometimes called the *time line* of cash management.

BOX 1.1

Time Line of Cash Management[a]

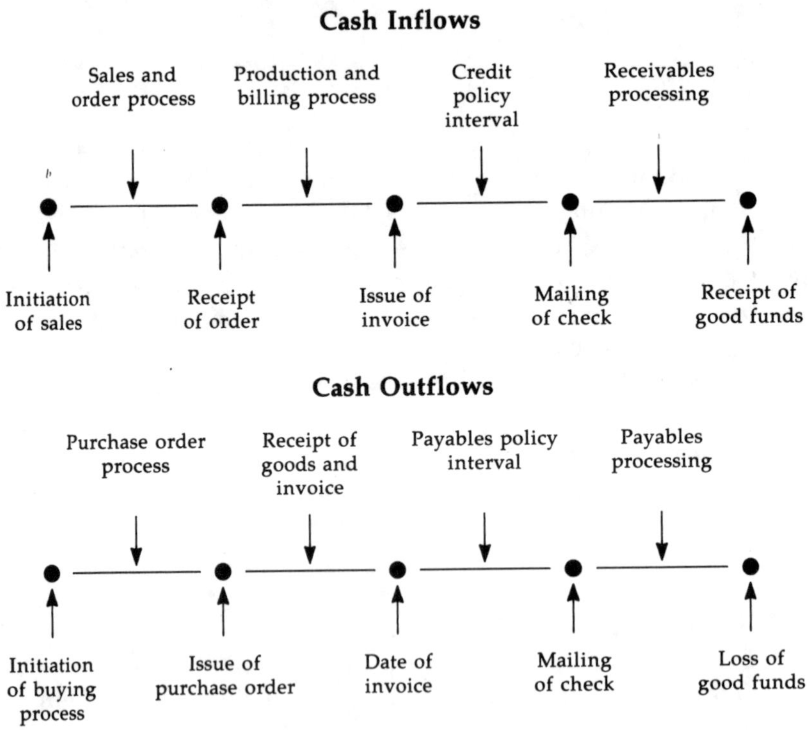

[a] Ned C. Hill, Gary W. Emery, and William L. Sartoris, *Essentials of Cash Management, A Study Guide* (Newton, CT: National Corporate Cash Management Assoc., 1985), p. 50.
[b] Dot indicates point in time.
[c] Horizontal line indicates duration.

What Motivated the Development of Cash Management?

The development of cash management as a discipline within the corporate treasury has been caused by five closely related trends:

1. Rising and fluctuating interest rates
2. Development of computers and electronic information technology
3. Growth of checks and other transaction volume in the banking system
4. Development of marketing and product management in banking
5. U.S. concern with productivity in response to foreign competitive challenges

Before exploring some of the current issues in cash management and the payments system, let us step back and review how the banking structure, the payments system, and cash management developed in the United States.

Evolution of the U.S. Payments System

On an average day in 1985, $1 trillion changed hands in the United States; $650 billion of that was transferred over the nation's electronic funds transfer networks. It would be difficult to envision our system of banking and commerce in the United States today without the payments system. We have become accustomed to a sound, elastic currency, a private but coordinated national banking system, and the ability to make payments reliably and safely throughout the country by electronic funds transfer. The banking infrastructure that underlies our payments system and cash management methods developed through a long evolutionary process starting in colonial times.[1]

The Federal Reserve Act of 1913 provided the foundation for our current banking system. As a compromise between centralization and decentralization, the Federal Reserve System was comprised of 12 regional reserve banks. Chartered national banks were required to become members and to comply with reserve requirements. The Federal Reserve Banks were empowered to issue currency backed by the gold and the commercial assets of the commercial banks, to conduct open market operations to expand and contract the nation's money supply, and to rediscount member bank securities. The system created elasticity in the money supply. Through the so-called *multiplier,* a loan from one bank would become a deposit in a second, providing the funds for a loan from the second bank that would become a deposit in the third, and so forth.

The Federal Reserve System provided the framework for the nation's payments mechanism. A national check collection and settlement system was established in 1915, and efforts began to eliminate nonpar checking (clearing and paying checks for a fee). In 1916, the Gold Settlement Fund, requiring the deposit of gold and gold certificates from the regional reserve banks was established. It provided a unified system of deposit accounts that allowed money transfers among member banks. By 1918, leased wires and a private Morse code system allowed interdistrict settlement every day. This marked the beginning of the Fed Wire. A teletype among member banks was installed in 1937.

[1] The Constitution gave Congress the power to mint coins and determine their value but did not allow the states to issue bills or notes. Its intent concerning a unified banking system was open to interpretation. The urban, mercantile interests of the Hamilton school and the agrarian, states-rights interests of the Jefferson school battled over that issue from then until the beginning of the twentieth century. The Bank of the United States in 1791 and the second Bank of the United States in 1816 represented attempts to establish a unified national currency, a regulator, and a lender of last resort. Neither survived beyond its original 20-year charter. For much of the nineteenth century, the nation's economy functioned with state-chartered banks that issued bank notes of varying quality.

The National Banking Act of 1863 established a system of national banks, with reserve requirements and a uniform currency of national bank notes backed by government bonds. It attempted to tax state bank notes out of existence. The state banks survived as checks were used more for commercial transactions and demand deposits were used more than bank notes to raise funds. The system was still inelastic. There was no mechanism to regulate money and credit. Country banks kept their reserves in reserve city banks, which in turn kept their reserves in central reserve city banks. In times of panic or even heavy seasonal demand, banks could meet demands for currency only by drawing down their reserves. The demands funneled into the large city banks and caused periodic failures. The failure of Jay Cooke & Co. precipitated the Panic of 1907, which motivated the appointment of the National Monetary Commission under the Aldrich–Vreeland Act the next year. The commission conducted a comprehensive study of the banking system, which was the basis for the Federal Reserve Act of 1913.

Problems in the 1930s motivated such legislation as the Glass–Steagall Act, which prohibited commercial banking and securities underwriting within one institution and provided for the establishment of the Federal Deposit Insurance Corporation. A system of par banking was extended throughout the country during that period. Member and nonmember banks had access to a nationwide deposit and clearing system.

As transaction volume grew in the 1960s, banks developed automated check processing equipment and magnetic ink character recognition (MICR) encoding for checks. Predictions of a checkless and cashless society were made. The Los Angeles and San Francisco clearing houses convened the Special Committee on Paperless Entries (SCOPE), the pilot for today's network of Automated Clearing Houses, in 1968. In 1969, the Federal Reserve installed its Culpepper (Virginia) Switch, a computer to link all of the Fed member banks for faster money transfer processing. In the same year, the New York Clearing House Association established the Clearing House Interbank Payments System (CHIPS), a computerized money transfer system to substitute for the huge volume of checks related to international transactions that were delivered by messenger from one New York City bank to another. The first Automated Clearing House (ACH) started to operate in California in 1972, and the National Association of Clearing Houses Associations (NACHA) was established in 1974.

The Payments System Today

The electronic payments system today consists of "settling" and "nonsettling" networks. Settling networks provide the mechanism for funds to move from one bank to another to settle net positions among those banks relating to customer money transfers and transactions for the banks' own accounts. Nonsettling networks are simply information systems used for money transfers. They are used by correspondent banks, which make money transfers by debiting and crediting accounts they maintain with each other. These are known as *book transfers*. One bank instructs the other to charge its account and pay the beneficiary or states that it is crediting the other bank's account on its books and instructs that bank to pay the beneficiary.

The Fed Wire is the primary wholesale electronic funds transfer (EFT) network in the United States. It is a settling network; payments received by a bank through this system are final and irrevocable. Although the Fed Wire was initially offered to only member banks, it became fee-based and open to all depository institutions under the Monetary Control Act of 1980.

CHIPS is the second largest wholesale EFT system in the number of payments, and the largest in dollar volume. It is a *net* settling network; net amounts due among the participants are settled by money transfers over the Fed Wire at the end of the working day. Because checks drawn on one New York City bank and deposited in another clear in one day, money transfers over CHIPS were in next day or "clearing house" funds until a new system of *same day settlement* was established in 1981. Originally, there were 12 New York Clearing House members in CHIPS, and all of the other Edge Act banking subsidiaries[2] and branches and agencies of foreign banks were associate members sponsored by one of the 12 settling members. In sponsoring a nonmember, a member agreed to arrange for settlement facilities in the event that the nonmember could not settle at the end of the day. There are now 143 members. Branches, agencies, and subsidiaries without the $250,000,000 in capital required for full membership are supported by a guarantee from their parent banks, or participate in the system as agents of their parents. Some physical presence in New York is required for participation in the system.

While the Fed Wire serves as the primary domestic payment system, CHIPS serves as the primary international system. Dollar transactions throughout the world are settled by money transfers sent from one New York bank to another over the CHIPS system. Ultimately, a currency can be held in only its country of domicile, and any dollar transaction must settle in the United States. A bank overseas can take dollar deposits and offer its customer dollar payment facilities only because that bank, in turn, has dollar deposits in the United States. A foreign exchange transaction involving the U.S. dollar will settle in New York whether that transaction is between two U.S. banks, a U.S. and a British bank, or an Italian and a Hong Kong bank. The dollar is the logical settlement currency between soft-currency countries. Accordingly, a letter of credit transaction between a Korean exporter and a Venezuelan importer would most likely settle between two banks in New York. All transactions in the huge Eurodollar market, which developed from dollars on deposit outside the United States, must ultimately settle in New York.

[2] An Edge Act subsidiary is (a) a subsidiary of a U.S. bank, or of a foreign bank operating in the United States, located outside that bank's principal state and engaged completely in international banking operations or (b) a holding company for a U.S. bank's overseas investments.

The Bank Wire was established in 1952 by nine New York and five Chicago banks to replace Telex and TWX for interbank communications. Until 1982, it was a nonsettling network and could be used for only book transfers among banks that maintained correspondent account relationships. In 1982, an adjunct settling system called Cash Wire was established. The Bank Wire ceased operation in early 1986 because of a decline in volume, increased use of a newer system, the Society for Worldwide Interbank Financial Telecommunications (SWIFT), for book transfers, and banks' unwillingness to commit the substantial investments required for automated interfaces, given the commitments already made to the other systems.[3]

The Society for Worldwide Interbank Financial Telecommunications is also a nonsettling communications network. It was established in 1973 as a nonprofit cooperative, primarily for international messages. Operation began in 1977; by 1981, 900 financial institutions in 39 countries were members. Message volume grew from 7 million in 1977 to 62 million in 1981; 110 U.S. banks are members. The United States is the largest originator of message traffic, followed by West Germany, the United Kingdom, and Italy. Ten percent of SWIFT's volume is among banks in the United States.

Development of Cash Management in the United States

Cash management evolved in the United States as the corporate treasury's art of dealing with the peculiarities of the U.S. banking system, mail system, and payments conventions.

Prior to 1950, interest rates were low, and the corporate treasurer did not have a large variety of external investment opportunities. There was more money in the banking system than there was loan demand. Banks funded their loans with interest-free demand deposits and invested the excess in safe, low-yielding government securities. Bankers competed with each other far less than they do today. They were highly selective in their corporate lending, motivating treasurers to keep large excess balances to protect credit facilities.

[3] Association of Reserve City Bankers, *Report on the Payments System* (Washington: 1982), 135.

The RCA corporation arranged a check collection system through Bankers Trust and the First National Bank of Chicago in 1947 more for administrative convenience than for concern over the time value of money. This was long before the term *lockbox* became common usage. It was designed to accelerate payments from dealers who were borrowing from RCA to finance their inventory of RCA products. It helped settle telephone arguments in which the borrower claimed "the check was in the mail."

In 1951, the Federal Reserve Board of Governors reached its historic "accord" with the U.S. Treasury Department and gained freedom in its open market operations. Heretofore, the Fed had been required to buy all government securities offered to it at minimum rates and thus kept prices from falling and yields from rising. With the accord, the Treasury lost its captive investor and had to start competing in the market for funds.

In the mid 1950s, the first postwar credit crunch and rising interest rates made the corporate treasurer more sensitive to the time value of money and the need to conserve bank balances. The European currencies became once again fully convertible, and higher yielding investment instruments began to compete for the U.S. investor's dollar. United States Treasury bills, which had dropped to 0.56% in 1958, did not go below 2.2% in 1960![4]

By 1960, cash had declined to 4.1% of sales for nonfinancial corporations from a level of 7.6% in 1946, according to a Federal Reserve Survey.[5] For the New York City banks, which had been the most prominent depositories for large corporations, the share of total deposits in the United States declined to 15% in 1960, down from 25% in 1941. The loan–deposit ratio of the New York City banks in 1960 was 63% in comparison to a 51% ratio for the "country" (nonreserve-city) banks. The need to buy funds and compete for deposits had come, and the Fed authorized the banks to issue negotiable certificates of deposit in 1961. Introduction of certificates of deposit (CDs) provided a new source of funds for banks and an investment instrument for corporations. It also marked the beginning of a new era of more complex bank liability management. No longer would the simple loan–deposit ratio be a sufficient measure of bank liquidity.

[4] James F. Lordan, *The Banking Side of Cash Management* (Boston: Financial Publishing, 1973), 25.

[5] Warren A. Law and M. Colyer Crum, "New Trend in Finance: The Negotiable C.D." in *Harvard Business Review* (Jan.–Feb. 1963), 158.

EXHIBIT 1

Short-Term Interest Rates

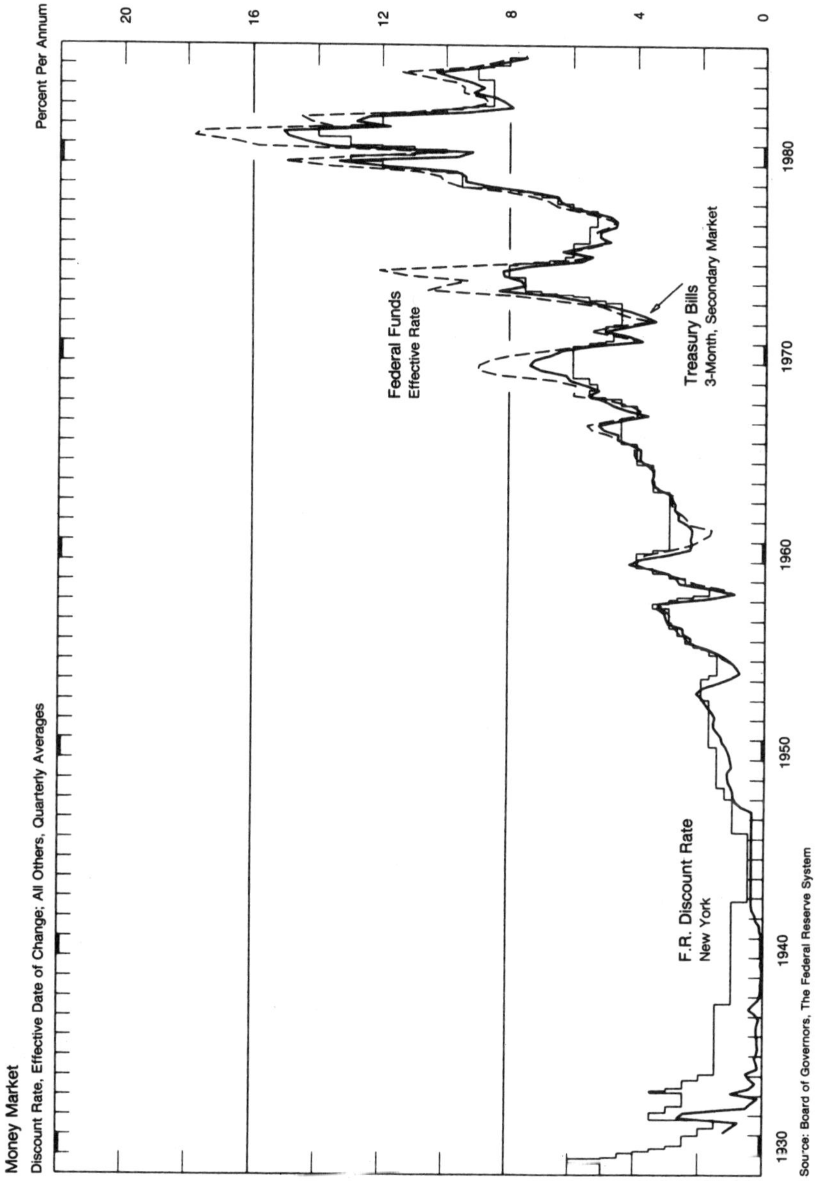

Interest rates continued to rise, as illustrated in Exhibit 1. Treasurers gained more confidence in their short-term investment capabilities. They diversified from low-yielding, liquid government securities into new instruments, such as municipal obligations, bankers' acceptances, commercial paper, and finance company paper. They started to finance the inventory of government bond dealers through overnight purchase–repurchase agreements, commonly known as *repos*.

The new breed of corporate treasurer worked cash harder, reduced bank balances, and demanded more bank services for the balances that remained. Banks that did not know the costs of their noncredit services had difficulty in justifying the balance compensation to support them. In an effort to hold their balances, they expanded their corporate services and developed more formal marketing programs.

Banking became less like a profession and more like a business with defined sales and profit objectives. The banks borrowed the product management discipline from the consumer goods manufacturers, started to standardize their services, and developed new ones. Product management in some banks was a separate function responsible for marketing, product planning, and profitability. Other banks implemented the product management philosophy by vesting the heads of such operations as letter of credit and lockbox with marketing and P&L responsibility. Corporate bankers became "calling officers" and "relationship managers." Sales became as important as credit in their job objectives. Specialized, noncredit sales groups emerged to support the more "generalist" calling officers.

Bank-operated lockboxes became more popular in the 1960s as corporate cash managers became more aware of both mail float and check-clearing float. Corporate bill collectors became more skilled at shortening mail time from the payer, while corporate bill payers became more skilled at lengthening it. Only in a country such as the United States, where it is customary to post a check rather than have cash in the hands of the customer within the agreed payment period, could such a tug-of-war take place! Lee Hecht, who was a professor at the University of Chicago prior to establishing the firm of Phoenix–Hecht, developed a model for studying mail times between one city and another. It was designed to optimize the location of bank lockboxes in relation to the concentration of bill payers' mailing points. His first formal study was conducted in 1968.

As check-clearing volume grew, a phenomenon called *slippage* became known. The Federal Reserve system gave credit for collected funds at the bank of deposit according to its standard schedule of one-, two-, and three-day collecting points, but in many cases, the Fed took longer to collect the check from the drawee bank. In the mid 1970s, a technique known as *remote disbursing* developed for taking advantage of slippage. Corporate billpayers mailed checks from obscure locations to maximize the time between the postmark on the envelope and the date the check was received by the payee and to take advantage of the Fed's delay in presenting checks for payment to country banks. When remote disbursing became widespread, the Fed voiced concern about banks and corporations using float at its own, and consequently at the public's, cost. It made policy statements against the practice and embarked on a campaign for check float reforms that were to be embodied in the Monetary Control Act of 1980.

The Depository Institutions Deregulation and Monetary Control Act of 1980, the most comprehensive banking legislation since the 1930s, made a number of changes destined to have an impact on bank services and prices for years to come. Because of concern over the cost to regional and smaller banks, the act did not affect corporate demand deposit accounts, but it provided for phasing out retail savings account interest rate ceilings under Regulation Q. It established uniform reserve requirements for all banks and expanded the trust, fiduciary, and lending powers of savings and loan associations. It empowered the Fed to start charging banks for such services as money transfers, check clearing, and ACH operations, which it had provided at no charge in the past, and the act mandated the Fed to eliminate float from the banking system to the extent possible.

As the Fed started to price its services, banks were motivated to improve their unit cost calculation for noncredit services and to consider dropping services for which market prices did not allow them a profit. To reduce float, the Fed speeded up its check collections with private couriers, hubs, and other improvements in its transportation network. The Fed's collection time began to rival those of correspondent banks with extensive direct-send networks. The regulator had become a competitor as well. When there were collection delays, the Fed started to charge back float to the banks on large dollar checks to reflect the actual availability of funds.

Remote disbursing gave way to *controlled disbursing,* which takes advantage of the Fed's presentment schedule in a different way. In a number of smaller cities, the final presentment of checks from the Fed was sufficiently early in the day so that a corporation could safely invest funds overnight knowing that there would be no additional charges against the account that day. As intrastate and interstate banking grew, a number of large banks offered controlled disbursing through their subsidiaries in smaller cities, funding the disbursing accounts from concentration accounts by money transfer or depository transfer check. The corporation had the advantages of both a large bank and a small bank. The Fed started in 1983 to "improve" its presentment schedule by making second presentments in the smaller cities later in the day as part of the float reduction program mandated by the Monetary Control Act. This appeared at first to be a threat to the existence of controlled disbursing, but the Fed developed a series of *payor services* to notify the banks electronically of the total amount of the last presentment and doing so sufficiently early in the day for the customer to realize the investment and control benefits of controlled disbursing.

In the mid-1970s, National Data Corporation (NDC), a company that processed inbound WATS line calls for Master Card franchisees, established a service through its time-sharing network for the automated creation of depository transfer checks. The NDC and General Electric Information Services Company (GEISCO) began to offer a service to gather and store bank balance and transaction information in standard formats that corporations could in turn retrieve using "dumb" computer terminals (without internal processing capabilities) connected through the telephone lines to the time-sharing computers. Banks made arrangements with such vendors as NDC and GEISCO for standard formatting of information and customer user numbers and sold the service as a package to their corporate and correspondent bank customers. One of the first was Chemical Bank in New York, which developed its own reporting service, called ChemLink, and later franchised the service to about 200 other banks in the United States and overseas under the name BankLink.

Use of the computer as the customer's "window to the bank" was the most important theme in cash management product development in the late 1970s and early 1980s. Multibank balance reporting was first offered in the United States and then in Europe and Asia. Numerous banks reported balance and transaction information to the time-sharing system of a vendor, such as GE, NDC, or ADP Network Services. That information was then consolidated into a daily report for the large corporate customer.

Small banks without the ability to transmit the information electronically could use a Telex or a touch-tone telephone or call in the information.

Customers began to get more detailed transaction information on more bank services. Banks offered such information as inbound money transfer amounts and descriptions on a "real-time" or a "frequent-batch-update" basis[6] during the working day, subject to final confirmation the next morning. Methods were developed for the customer to initiate money transfers using the terminal in his or her office. Procedures soon followed for more complex transactions such as letter of credit applications.

The popularity and corporate adoption of the IBM Personal Computer inspired banks and software firms to develop the so-called "treasury workstation." Software was developed for corporations to telephone and retrieve information from their banks automatically, consolidating information in the various bank formats into easy-to-read reports. The PC quickly replaced the paper spread sheet. Corporations could buy programs or develop their own to keep track of bank balances, borrowings, and investments and to forecast receipts and disbursements. The treasury function became less dependent on the mainframe and the corporate systems staff.

Time-sharing expenses had always been high, and the so-called "packet-switching" networks, such as Tymnet, allowed cheaper transmission of information directly from the bank to the customer. By 1984, banks started installing their own fault tolerant computers (with built-in backup) to store the information that had been stored for customer retrieval in the time-sharing networks.

Banks installed new automated lockbox systems with optical character recognition capabilities, which updated the customer's accounts receivable files electronically and separated and deposited checks more quickly to meet critical availability deadlines. As mail time and bank processing time analysis became more refined, similar methodologies were applied to disbursing. Security Pacific Bank developed a "disbursement network" to optimize disbursement mailing points and banks by vendor/payee. Valutech of Santa Ana, California, went a step further and developed software for optimizing both the check-mailing point and the

[6] The term *real-time* means that the information file is updated at the same time the transaction is entered into one of the bank's processing systems. Many banks do not provide real-time systems but update their customer information files with frequent batch transmissions during the working day.

disbursing bank for each check. Specialized printers made by the Troy Corporation, also of Santa Ana, print the bank's name and MICR encoding for each check on blank check stock.

As the technology advanced for collecting and disbursing checks, electronic payment alternatives were developed as well. Banks promoted corporate trade payments through the ACH. Industry groups developed netting systems to reduce payment volume and embarked on pilot projects to integrate order processing, shipping, and accounts receivable management and payment in a standardized electronic business data interchange system. Corporations saw the efficiency of electronic payments on one hand but were reluctant to give up disbursement float on the other. Through inertia, the paper check was destined to be used in corporate payments for a long time to come.

In the early 1980s, record high interest rates made cash management more important than ever before. Stories of messengers flying from one coast to another to present large checks for payment were not unusual. Some corporations considered treating cash management as a profit center. Mastering the new computerized products, getting information from all of the banks on time, pulling funds in from some bank accounts while replenishing others, making required disbursements, and deciding on investment instruments and maturities was more than enough to keep the cash manager busy. The corporate treasurer was, at the same time, straining to learn a host of techniques designed for coping with an unprecedented era of interest rate volatility, such as swaps, futures, options, caps, and collars. The days of arranging major debt packages and just letting them sit had passed. There was no longer any permanence in the liability structure. Ethics and the law as they applied to cash management were not knowingly being ignored. They were just not in the forefront of the treasurer's and the cash manager's minds as they strove to keep up with the pace of constantly evolving techniques and products.

Summary and Conclusions

The Art of Cash Management Corporations developed ways of coping with the peculiar features of the banking system, the payments system, bill-paying conventions, and the mail system in the United States in order to minimize idle cash.

Float Delays in the mail and check clearing time became a resource for the corporate bill payer to maximize and for the bill collector and the

Federal Reserve System to minimize. Banks developed lockboxes for the bill collectors while the Federal Reserve began efforts to reduce float in the system.

Rising Interest Rates Increased sensitivity to the time value of money further motivated cash management. It was caused by rising and fluctuating interest rates, which were in turn caused primarily by inflation. The interest rate history chart in Exhibit 1 provides a graphic explanation of why cash management became necessary.

Erosion of Bank Demand Deposits Corporate treasurers found interest-earning short-term investments. One of those investment vehicles was the certificate of deposit, which the banks developed in the early 1960s to fund themselves in place of the diminishing demand deposits.

Technology Banks offered new cash management services, such as computerized information and transaction initiation, Automated Clearing House payments, electronic update of accounts receivable, and treasury workstations. Offering up-to-date cash management services became a requirement for banks that wanted to do business with large corporations.

Deregulation Banks were allowed to enter new areas of business while other institutions, such as brokerage firms and money market funds, were allowed to compete with the banks for deposits.

2 E. F. Hutton: Catalyst for Defining the Ground Rules

On May 2, 1985, E. F. Hutton, the nation's fifth largest stock brokerage firm, pleaded guilty to 2000 felony counts of intentional mail and wire fraud. Hutton was fined $2,000,000, the maximum allowed by the law for that number of counts, and the steepest ever in the history of white-collar crime enforcement. The firm also reserved $8,000,000 for the most comprehensive program of restitution ever developed in a criminal case. Additionally, the government required Hutton to pay $750,000 to cover costs of the investigation.

A Case History

At the core of the case was a massive check-kiting scheme that artificially inflated bank balances. In effect, Hutton deceived banks into giving it unsecured, interest-free, short-term loans. The Justice Department considered the Hutton practices potentially dangerous to smaller banks and an extreme example of the float-creating practices that had been criticized by the Federal Reserve System in recent years.

Although the Justice Department believed that two unidentified individuals were primarily responsible in a criminal sense for the cited activities, it chose not to prosecute those individuals. Rather than engage in the lengthy, juried court case that would have been required, it chose to reach an immediate settlement. It was able to impose stiff penalties and convey an important message to the public without delay.

The inquiry was triggered by a $8,100,000 check that the Genesee County Bank of Batavia, New York, refused for insufficient funds. The Justice Department worked with the New York State Banking Commission and the Federal Reserve Bank of New York from May 1982 to April 1985. The investigation was based in Harrisburg, Pennsylvania to limit the possibility of publicity.

The criminal offenses cited by the Justice Department were:

> Drawing down arbitrary and excessive amounts, unrelated to and far in excess of customer deposits, on accounts in smaller country banks and covering the resulting overdrafts with checks drawn on New York zero-balance accounts. Hutton was able to take advantage of the float from slow-clearing times with checks both deposited in, and drawn on, the country banks. The firm took advantage of uncollected funds in banks that did not have the systems to track them and were not accustomed to the type of banking and customer relationships in which such practices would be suspected.

> Deliberately moving funds through "chains" of banks as part of an elaborate scheme to delay collection artificially and create float. Hutton had taken advantage of the inefficiencies in the check clearing system wherein the Fed, in accordance with its standard availability schedule, often gave the depositor credit for collected funds before the checks were collected from the drawee bank. Those are the inefficiencies that motivated remote disbursing. An illustration of chaining is provided in Exhibit 2.

EXHIBIT 2

The folling diagram illustrates normal concentration and chaining. Let us assume that branches of a brokerage firm receive funds each day that are in turn remitted to the firm's concentration account. Under normal concentration procedures, the branch would remit funds directly to the concentration bank by depository transfer check, through the ACH, or by instructing the local bank to make a money transfer. If it were creating a depository transfer check for deposit in the concentration bank, the branch office would make the amount greater than the available balance in the local bank on that day, anticipating funds that will become available by the time the check deposited in the concentration bank is presented to the local bank for payment. It might even draw on uncollected funds based on a prior agreement with the bank to compensate for recent balances above the agreed-on average.

Normal Concentration

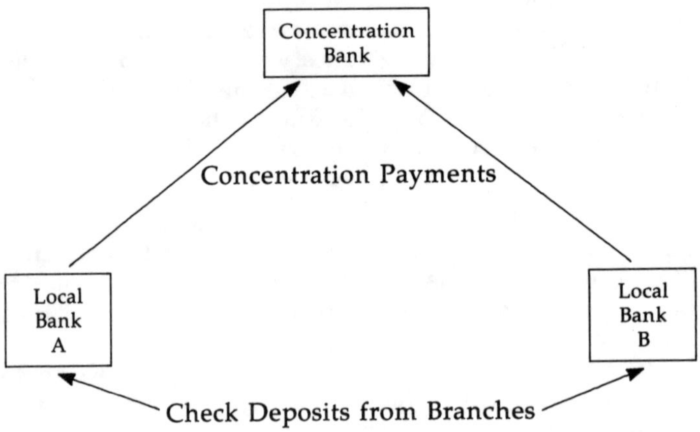

Chaining would involve remitting funds to the concentration bank through a circuitous route to take advantage of slippage. For example, Branch Office A might arrange to have a check drawn on its account in Bank A and deposited in Bank B. On the same day, a payment would be made from Bank B to the concentration bank. The amount of that concentration payment would take the deposit from Bank A and anticipated check-clearing times into account. According to the Fed's schedule, the deposit is available in two days. However, let us assume that because of slippage, the Fed takes three days to present the check and collect funds from Bank A. The brokerage firm would have use of the funds in both banks for one day.

Chaining

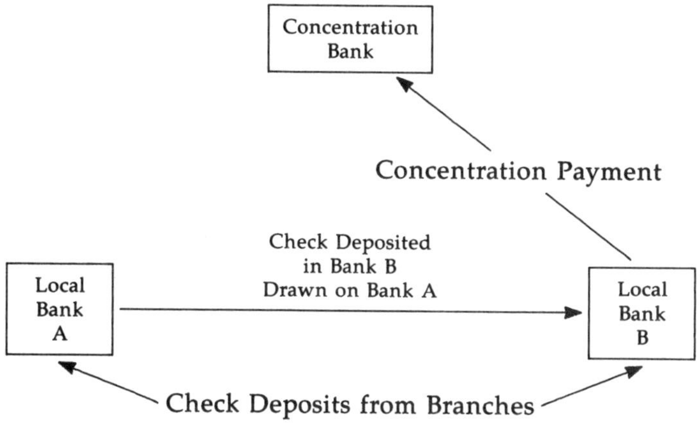

The laws cited in the plea agreement were two broadly worded and closely related sections of the United States Code, Title 18, entitled "Crimes and Criminal Procedure." They are listed verbatim in Appendix I. Section 1341, *Mail Fraud,* defines as a criminal act any scheme to defraud or obtain money or property by means of false or fraudulent pretenses, as well as the unlawful use of any counterfeit coin, obligation, or security in which the U.S. mails are used. The purpose of the law is to prohibit attempts to defraud by any form of misrepresentation. Section 1343, entitled *Fraud by Wire, Radio and Television,* is patterned in Section 1341. Wire is construed to include telephone.

Until the Hutton incident, there had been virtually no case law pertaining to contemporary cash management. The most relevant cases had been check-kiting schemes prosecuted under Section 1341, *Mail Fraud;* Section 1343, *Fraud by Wire, Radio, and Television* (fewer in number because it is a more recent law); and Section 1014, *Loan and Credit Applications; Renewals and Discounts.* Section 1014 covers false statements or reports and willfully overvaluing land, property, or securities for the purpose of influencing any bank insured by the Federal Deposit Insurance Corporation.

The legal parallels between the check-kiting cases prosecuted under Section 1341 and the Hutton case are clear. Only the technology had changed. Evidence of a *scheme designed to defraud* and use of the mails are the two requirements for a conviction. Proof of actual injury or success in the scheme was not required. In most of the check-kiting cases, as with Hutton, *knowingly deceiving* the banks was the primary legal issue. Use of the mails in any way by the accused in the course of his or her scheme put these check-kiting cases under the scope of Section 1341.

In October 1984, a new *bank fraud* statute, Section 1344, was modeled directly on the mail fraud statute. It proscribes the use of any scheme or artifice to defraud a federally chartered or insured financial institution or to obtain funds, securities, or any other assets under control of such an institution. Section 1344 was designed partly to cover any loopholes in which mail, wire, radio, or television was not involved. For example, some of the check-kiting cases in which courier services were used could not be prosecuted under the mail fraud statute. The new section was enacted while the Hutton investigation was underway and therefore could not be applied to the alleged offenses that occurred between July 1980 and December 1982.

Two decisions in the early 1980s precluded the Justice Department's opportunity to prosecute for check kiting under sections 1341 and 1343. The decision in *United States* v. *Williams*, 458 U.S. 279 (1982) states that a check "does not make any representation as to the state of the petitioner's bank balances...nor is it an overvalued security." In *United States* v. *Frankel*, 721 F.2d 917 (3d Cir. 1983), the Court relied on the Williams case to conclude that a check kite could not be charged under the "false pretenses, representations, and promises" clause of 1341 because a check was not a representation. Therefore, the Justice Department had to take a different approach under 1341 and 1343. It had to argue that Hutton had misrepresented to its banks that deposit accounts were established only to handle customer funds, when those accounts were really intended to process huge overdraft checks. That approach was not easy because many of the victimized banks had been negligent in not calling attention to the overdrafts and use of uncollected funds. Some had even terminated their relationships with Hutton when they discovered how they were being treated but had not notified any law enforcement authorities.

The Justice Department complained that the *Williams* and *Frankel* decisions tied their hands in prosecuting check kiting and similar offenses and began efforts that resulted in enactment of the bank fraud statute, Section 1344. The Hutton case occurred in the window between the *Williams* and *Frankel* decisions and the enactment of Section 1344.

At the same time that it handed down the criminal penalties, the Justice Department "permanently restrained and enjoined" Hutton under civil law, 18 U.S.C 1345, *Injunctions against Fraud* from seven specific practices:

1. Failing to disclose and describe, in writing, to each bank or financial institution with which they maintained a depository account, all money management techniques or practices in connection with, not without limitation, the concentration and intracompany transfers of funds
2. Drawing down arbitrary amounts unrelated to customer funds deposits from depository accounts and thereafter covering such drawdowns by checks drawn on other Hutton accounts
3. Transferring funds between successive banks "to inflate the funds drawn down so that they exceed the amount of customer funds originally deposited" and using formulas for drawdowns by which the amount of customer funds deposited was "excessively multiplied or otherwise arbitrarily increased," and thereby exploiting opportunities for delayed clearing times of items deposited into branch depository banks
4. Causing uncollected funds to be withdrawn by any means, including by the use of a multiplier formula, in which there was not a written agreement or consent from the bank concerned
5. Withdrawing funds in excess of those received from customers or institutional clients at any time, by any means, including the use of a multiplier or formula, unless there were written agreements or consents authorizing such withdrawals
6. Creating float by retarding, delaying, or obstructing the clearing of checks deposited in bank branches or regional depository accounts
7. Issuing checks in identical amounts in different banks and cross depositing those checks, thereby causing each bank to certify next-day opening balances in their account

The 18 U.S.C. 1345 injunctive provision was enacted into law in 1984, and this was the first time it was used. Unlike 1344, which applied to prosecution for wrongdoing in the past, 1345 applied to the future. Hutton was not prosecuted for having followed these practices in the past but was put on notice that those practices would be considered criminal in the future.

Shortly after Hutton pleaded guilty to the above-cited felony counts, several banks encountered encoding and printing errors on Hutton's checks. When the MICR encoding cannot be read by a bank's high-speed check-processing equipment during a normal run, that check is sorted out and processed by hand the next day. The clearing process is delayed by a day, and the maker of the check gains the float. The practice was not cited by the Justice Department, but it was included in the investigation conducted by Griffin B. Bell. His staff interviewed Hutton personnel in money management, cash control, forms control, purchasing, accounting services, and internal audit, as well as Hutton's outside check printer and representatives from the banks concerned. They concluded that there were instances of printer error, human error in preparing printer specifications, lack of timely notification of problems by the banks, and inadequate controls within the Hutton organization. However, they concluded that the check-encoding problems were not the result of deliberate efforts to create clearing delays "to the banks' detriment or to Hutton's benefit."

Finally, the Securities and Exchange Commission conducted an investigation later in 1985 into six other alleged policies and practices. It commissioned Touche Ross & Co. to conduct an investigation into whether those policies and practices conformed to the federal securities laws, the rules of the National Association of Securities Dealers and other self-regulatory organizations, and a broker/dealer's fiduciary duty to its customers. Those practices were:

1. Discouraging customers from requesting automatic dividend payments, thus keeping money in customer accounts on which Hutton, and not the customer, earned interest
2. Maximizing the use of customers' free credit balances
3. Discouraging customers from requesting check payments from local bank accounts
4. Encouraging customer participation in such investments as short sales or margin accounts, which generated interest income for Hutton
5. Substituting checks drawn on Hutton accounts for checks received from customers in payment for investments, thereby channeling funds through Hutton bank accounts
6. Collecting or attempting to collect customer funds prior to the settlement date for investment transactions

Touche Ross & Co. found a number of the relevant rules and legal standards that applied to these practices to be imprecise. It said that a number of the issues examined involved long-standing practices that were well known to the SEC and the self-regulatory organizations and pointed out that only recently had there been focus on whether some of the practices were appropriate. Touche Ross & Co. found no evidence of sales practices to generate interest income for Hutton, to discourage customers from requesting automatic dividend payments in cash accounts, or to encouraging them to request such payments in margin accounts. It found no evidence of policies or practices to encourage settlement prior to settlement. Disbursements from out-of-state were the result of a single-bank disbursement system, not a deliberate remote-disbursing policy. Hutton was in compliance with regulatory requirements for notifying customers of the availability of their free credit balances. Touche Ross & Co. recommended that Hutton improve the disclosure of its practices on the payment of dividends and interest to customers with cash or margin accounts and its practices concerning the substitution of Hutton checks for customer checks. Thus, the need for clarification of the rules was more evident than Hutton's violation of them in this case. Nonetheless, the fact that the SEC cited these practices is useful information, especially in a field such as corporate cash management where not very much is explicitly defined in the law.

The Bank Restitution Program

As part of its agreement with the Justice Department, Hutton entered into a comprehensive restitution program with all of its banks. The program entailed a review of all account activity and related service charges from July 1, 1980 to December 31, 1982. Hutton was required to reimburse each bank for all undercompensation based on the broker call rate for the month concerned, adjusted for reserve requirements. While carrying out the restitution program, Hutton hired a new senior vice president, Paul Beehler, to design and implement a comprehensive new treasury operations and banking relations program. Beehler had previously been in charge of Arthur Young & Company's treasury consulting services.

Analysis

How Hutton's Cash Management Practices Developed: Incentives and Organizational Structure

Money management specialists in Hutton's New York headquarters designed a system for Hutton's extensive branch network and 400-odd banking relationships that originally, on paper, would have been considered within the bounds of accepted practice. Because of the size of the branch network and the decentralized organizational structure, Hutton used regional concentration banks as well as a central concentration bank in New York. In effect, Hutton operated its own manual depository transfer check system. Branch offices telephoned the amounts of customer deposits to regional headquarters, including the amounts of immediately available funds. Regional headquarters deposited checks in regional concentration banks drawn on each branch banking account. The New York office used the same procedure to draw in funds from regional concentration banks. The amounts of the concentration checks were intended to be calculated to anticipate the actual availability of each day's deposits in the drawee bank. If Hutton anticipated that a concentration check would be presented to the drawee bank in two days, then the amount of that concentration check was theoretically based on the amount of collected funds that would be in Hutton's account in the drawee bank at that time.

The actual use of the system diverged radically from the original plan. The line branch managers who used it reported to regional vice presidents who, in turn, reported to the president. They had only an indirect functional relationship with the money management people in the New York operations staff who designed the system. The money management staff had neither the access nor the incentives to monitor the day-to-day performance of the system. The branch managers not only had control of the daily cash concentration procedures, but a built-in incentive to abuse the system. For internal reporting purposes, branch profits included interest income earned, and the branch managers' compensation included 10% of branch profits.

Questions Raised by the Hutton Case

What was the meaning of the Hutton case? Was it inevitable that someone would push the system too far as cash management became more sophisticated and the financial stakes grew higher? Were the Hutton cash management practices an example of what was happening throughout the corporate community or simply highly unusual cases of fraud? How applicable was the Hutton indictment to other corporations? Where did the Justice Department intend to go from here? What was legal and what was not? Was some type of future legislation on the subject of cash management in the offing? These were some of the questions raised when the Hutton case became public. For a while at least, cash management became a popular subject of discussion in the boardroom and throughout the business community rather than an esoteric practice known only to a few technicians.

The Hutton incident was a watershed in the history of cash management. The early 1980s environment of unprecedented high interest rates encouraged banks to develop new products and corporations to learn new techniques. Corporations were concerned with "bottom line" impact, and some considered making the cash management function a profit center. Playing the cash management game became an ethos. This environment encouraged cash managers to push and test the system. There seemed to be little reason not to. There had not been much discussion of the legal and ethical boundaries. An incident such as Hutton was needed as a catalyst to bring these issues to the attention of the corporate community. In our survey, we discussed the legal boundaries with the Justice Department. We polled the corporate community on the ethical boundaries. We also asked corporations to what extent they had reevaluated their cash management organization and procedures in light of Hutton.

Legal Guidelines for the Corporate Cash Manager

We discussed the legal message that should be conveyed to the corporate community with Peter Clark, a member of the Justice Department's Fraud Section in Washington who worked on the Hutton case during most of its final year. Based on these discussions, we believe that there is a rule of reason that should help define the boundary between legal and illegal and should not be difficult for the corporate cash manager to discern. With Hutton, as with the long history of check-kiting cases prosecuted under sections 1341 and 1343, the primary issue is deception—one party taking unfair advantage of the other.

Take the example of one large corporate buyer paying an equally sophisticated vendor. The buyer uses a disbursement network to extend mail and bank-clearing float and discovers that he or she can get away with consistently paying three days after terms expire. The vendor should be able to detect what is going on and may be able to rotate its lockbox locations just as fast. These practices may be just short of, or just beyond, the boundary of accepted cash management practices. Clark points out that a scheme designed to defraud is generally hard to prove in a disbursement case. Far more blatant would be a system to falsify postmarks and to date checks five days earlier than the date the check is cut. Another example might be a brokerage firm consistently not making required payments to retail customers until those customers call and ask for them.

Finally, in today's legal environment, Clark refers to chaining as a kamikaze practice.

The seven practices enjoined under Section 1345 could be construed as criminal practices for another corporation in the future. Some exception may be allowed to the injunction under Section 1345 as it applies to written agreements between corporations and banks. Clark believes that verbal agreements are acceptable but cautions that those agreements are harder to prove in court. The issue is of interest because some banks are reluctant to commit to agreements in writing concerning overdrafts and uncollected funds, preferring to have more flexibility and to make accommodations for customers on a case-by-case basis.

Cash Management Legislation

Aside from the Hutton practices enjoined by the Justice Department, the practices cited by the SEC, and a few local laws—such as one in Louisiana requiring payrolls to be from in-state banks and fully funded the day they are released and requirements that brokerage firms pay from in-state banks—there does not appear to be any political force to create cash management legislation in reaction to Hutton. Unlike consumer banking issues, such as delayed availability for checks deposited that are drawn on out-of-town banks, there is not an aggrieved group within the world of corporate cash management pushing for such legislation.

Corporate Reaction to E. F. Hutton

Reaction to the Hutton affair within the corporate treasury function varied. In general, the Hutton practices were considered very unusual and way beyond normal corporate practice. But whether or not corporations were concerned about the legality and ethics of their cash management practices, a number of financial officers used the Hutton incident as a good excuse to review their policies and procedures in this changing and still relatively new discipline.

In many corporations, there were questions from top management about E. F. Hutton; in some, there were questions from the board. Often, the treasury function answered those questions informally, confirming that the company was not following any of the practices cited in the Hutton incident. One treasurer prepared a detailed memorandum for the

CFO just in case questions were asked during the forthcoming board meeting, but no questions were asked.

Of the 833 members responding to the NCCMA's recent survey, 28% instituted internal review procedures in reaction to Hutton, 32% provided explanations of their systems or activities to senior management, and 48% took no action at all. In the FERF questionnaire and interviews, we asked corporations how their organizational structure, codes of conduct, objectives, and measurement systems were changing. Corporations were asked how their criteria for evaluating bank relationships were changing and how their collection, concentration, disbursement, and investment practices were changing.

Cash Management Policies and Codes of Conduct

Forty-five percent of our respondents report that they have a written policy on cash management. Of those that do, the majority report that it has been reviewed by the CFO, the treasurer, and both the internal and external auditors. Board of directors or audit committee reviews were mentioned by 30% of the companies with sales below $1 billion but by only 10% of companies with sales above $1 billion. Periodic reviews of the cash management policy are most often conducted by the treasurer, followed by internal auditors for 30% of the companies, external auditors for 20%, and the board and the audit committee for 10% each. Internal counsel is involved in 20% of the cases, but in only a few cases has external counsel been involved. One large company explained the mechanics of controlled disbursing in detail to the legal staff in light of possible Justice Department misunderstanding of the difference between controlled disbursing and remote disbursing.

The written policies contain a mission statement in the majority of cases. One-third of the respondents report that the statement covers such quantitative goals as cost savings, interest earnings, or bank fees, and a third say that it covers controversial cash management practices. A number wrote that the statement covers investment guidelines, and some mentioned borrowing policies, wire transfer and concentration policies, and guidelines for handling bank accounts.

Benson K. Woo, director, Worldwide Banking and U.S. Cash Management for General Motors wrote, "Although no written policy on cash management exists, a general policy in terms of ethical behavior controls how G.M. manages its cash. We are the largest industrial in the

U.S. and as such will never employ abusive practices. We are sensitive to adverse publicity."

Mario Goveia, manager of Domestic Banking and Treasury Administration for Champion Spark Plug, wrote, "We have an open, honest proactive and assertive relationship with all of our banks. While we look out for our own best interests in the long run, this includes compensating them fairly, not over or under. Their confidence in this philosophy and style enables them to give us the flexibility we need without demanding noncredit written agreements." Goveia added that personal working relationships and trust are essential in the formation of a corporate–bank relationship and can help keep it together when disputes between the institutions arise.

Gordon L. Lacey, director of Cash Management and Financial Services in 3M Corporation's Treasury Division, has recently developed a mission statement and was kind enough to provide it for the purpose of this study.

BOX 2.1

3M Corporation Cash Management Mission Statement

To operate a world-class, professional cash management organization to meet the cash requirements of 3M operations by positioning investments in approved securities, or by borrowing as required, to receive and disburse funds efficiently, and to minimize operating costs.

Principles

1. To incorporate the highest levels of professionalism, innovation, and technology into 3M's cash management practices

2. To work closely with banks and financial organizations and 3M's divisions, subsidiaries, and staff departments to provide highly responsive service and a keen awareness of sophisticated cash management practices

3. To accurately forecast sources and uses of funds and take appropriate actions to ensure availability of sufficient cash to meet day-to-day and long-term needs at the best price

4. To establish and monitor a network to receive, process, and concentrate monies owed to 3M as rapidly and efficiently as possible

5. To establish and monitor systems that ensure timely payment to vendors and employees and to maximize the benefits of legitimate float without taking improper advantage of system or mechanical delays
6. To invest excess cash according to policies established by the 3M board of directors with the objective of providing appropriate levels of safety, liquidity and yield, in that order
7. To provide accurate, timely, and dependable accounting records related to 3M's operations
8. To provide ongoing review of financial services vendors and internal controls to ensure sufficient security for the protection of 3M's cash, securities, and investments
9. To fairly compensate banks and financial vendors for services provided

Procedures Document

Fifty-five percent of our respondents have a written document describing cash management procedures. Almost all of those report that it is used by internal auditors in their periodic review of the treasury function. This is of interest in light of comments that the kind of practices followed by Hutton should have been caught by its auditors and that some auditors do not look beyond the accounting entries. A number of corporations use the document as a training manual, and some have used it for job evaluation and rating purposes. One large company found its manual to be a useful reference point in coordinating its cash management procedures with those of a large acquired company.

Review with Banks

Just over half of the companies that replied, and generally the larger ones, have felt compelled to review their cash management procedures with their banks to ensure that they conform with generally accepted practice. In most cases, reviews have been informal and initiated by corporations. In only a few cases has the discussion been followed by a written agreement. Some companies have chosen to go on record by writing a letter to their banks documenting their procedures, with the assumption that no reply is tacit approval.

Charles Clayton, manager, Banking and Cash Management for Shell Oil Company, agreed to share Shell's cash management policy and standards letter, which it recently sent to all of its banks.

BOX 2.2

Cash Management Policy and Standards Letter

(Date)

(Bank name)

Dear ________ :

Recent publicity on corporate cash management practices suggests the need to inform you of Shell's cash management policy and standards. For purposes of this letter, reference to Shell encompasses also banking arrangements on behalf of its subsidiaries and other related operations.

It is Shell's policy to conduct its cash management activities totally within applicable laws and consistent with the highest ethical standards. Its cash management practices are not unlike those advocated by leading cash management banks and are believed to be widely used by other corporations with efficient cash management programs. Shell values its relationship with its banks and expects these associations to be profitable for both parties. To ensure compliance with its policy objectives, the company has established specific standards for its cash management operations which are described below.

If there are two or more Shell accounts at a particular bank, *collected* balances at such bank are aggregated and administered on a combined basis. It is our understanding that this netting of negative balances against positive balances satisfies bank examiners and is permitted under Regulation D. Shell administers its banking relationships based on an "average collected balance objective" which is calculated over a twelve-month period from May 1 of each year to April 30 of the following year. Shell's cash management procedures are expected to achieve a positive average collected balance with every bank by the end of each month for such month.

In order to achieve an average collected balance objective by the end of each month, it may become necessary to delay or to accelerate the movement of funds to concentration banks. When movement of funds is accelerated in order to recapture previously excessive collected balances, Shell will only advance against expected deposits so that the bank will not be overdrawn on a ledger basis. If other arrangements are found to be necessary, Shell will discuss the matter with the bank and obtain its prior concurrence as an exception to our normal procedures. For operational efficiency, Shell uses controlled disbursement banks where the Federal Reserve presents checks no more than twice a day before noon. These banks are used solely to help ABC better manage its daily cash position by knowing the exact amount of daily funding required.

It is Shell's intent to maintain a positive *ledger* balance in every bank account by the end of each business day. Nevertheless, overdrafts may occur from time to time as when caused by human error, systems failure, delayed clearings, or other random events. To eliminate an unexpected overdraft, Shell will—as soon as practical after notification by the bank—delay the movement of current deposits to concentration accounts and/or wire-transfer in the amount necessary to cover the overdraft.

Shell's cash management standards specifically forbid the following:

— Banking relationships with ongoing negative average collected balances or accounts with negative ledger balances

— Designing or maintaining cash management systems or procedures solely for the purpose of creating or enhancing float as, for example, through use of remote banks or multiple transfers

— Designing or maintaining cash management systems or procedures that obstruct or delay the normal check-clearing process

Shell's policy is to compensate its banks fairly for services rendered either through fees or by maintaining compensating balances or combination of both. With compensating balance arrangements, over or undercompensation in any one month is adjusted during the following month(s).

Whereas the primary purpose of this letter is to inform you of Shell's standards for its cash management, I would appreciate it if you would inform me of any instance which causes you to believe that we may not have lived up to these standards. Furthermore, if and when you feel that any serious cash management problem is not being resolved by Shell representatives responsibly and in good faith, I ask that you let me know as soon as possible.

Please acknowledge receipt of this letter by signing below and sending a copy of the signed letter to me.

Shell appreciates your attention to this matter and values highly the fine relationship we have with your bank.

Very Truly Yours,

Assistant Treasurer

Enclosure

Received and Acknowledged by: ________

Agreements with Banks in Writing

Consistent with the previously cited remarks of Peter Clark, most companies believe that the Justice Department injunction requiring Hutton to disclose its cash management procedures *in writing* to each of its banks, and not to draw on uncollected funds at any time *without written agreement*, applies only to Hutton. Some that we interviewed believe that a regular account analysis, comparing average balances required with balances maintained, documenting fees, and showing evidence of a means for making up balance deficiencies—with either balances or fees—is de facto evidence of an agreement between the company and the bank.

Seventy percent of the agreements, whether written or verbal, include an opinion that the company's cash management procedures are acceptable as far as that bank is concerned. Seventy percent include agreements concerning permissibility of overdrafts and uncollected funds and compensation for same required by the bank. Fifty percent cite an agreement concerning credit for excess balances. Thirty-five percent cite a bank opinion that cash management procedures are consistent with current legal and ethical guidelines. Very few companies that have requested a review of their cash management procedures have encountered any resistance from their banks. About half of the companies that have not reviewed the legality and ethics of their cash management procedures have plans to do so. Most of them expect the agreements to be verbal.

One-third of the banks that replied to the questionnaire indicated that they had conducted a formal review and agreed with the cash management procedures of some of their customers. Ninety percent said that they would be willing to do so if asked. Responsibility for such an agreement usually rests with the head of the cash management department but often in conjunction with the relationship manager. Some bankers have given briefings to corporations on the details of the Hutton affair, and one bank has conducted all-day seminars on cash management for corporate auditors.

Review of Procedures

About half of the respondents changed some of their cash management policies or procedures within the last year. An internal treasury function review was the reason most often cited. A substantial number also cited recent publicity of unethical cash management procedures, discussions with their banks, discussions with their internal auditors, and bank consulting studies. Only a few changed any of their procedures because of discussions with their external auditors or lawyers. Procedures run the gamut of treasury operations—chaining the location of disbursing banks, reviewing concentration procedures, improving documentation, reviewing bank ledger overdraft and uncollected funds policies, centralizing disbursement and other treasury functions, and consolidating the number of banking relationships. The procedures that were changed appear to have been more in the categories of efficiency and control and less in the area of questionable practices discovered as a result of the Hutton affair. Only a small number reported changing their check-mailing points.

Some treasurers and cash managers said that they wanted to make sure they were "in the pack" in their procedures and not "on the leading edge." Although they expressed confidence that their cash management procedures fell within legal and ethical guidelines, they were interested in better defining what the ground rules were and whether those rules had changed as a result of the Hutton incident.

BOX 2.3

To survey cash managers' opinions, 10 controversial cash management practices were included in the questionnaire for comment. The percentage of the 197 respondents that considered each practice to be either unethical or subject to possible legal problems in the future is:

— Altering checks so that they cannot be processed by banks' high-speed equipment	87%
— Drawing on uncollected funds in banks that do not have sophisticated float-tracking systems	70
— Drawing on uncollected funds when not covered by an agreement with a bank	63
— Rotating disbursement points to deoptimize vendors' lockbox configurations	39
— Anticipatory drafting	33

— Sending checks to a company' office rather than to a designated lockbox	33
— Paying East Coast vendors from West Coast banks and/or mailing points and vice versa	32
— Overdrafts at any time	30
— Any systems designed to extend disbursing float	21
— Uncollected funds at any time	12

Very few of the respondents volunteered any other unethical or legally questionable procedures in the space provided. The opinions on cash management ethics do not appear to vary much by industry or size of company. A speaker at a recent convention suggested as a guideline for acceptability any procedure that a corporation would not mind having identified on the front page of the *Wall Street Journal*. Paul Beehler, who was appointed senior vice president, Financial Operations at Hutton shortly after the plea was made public last summer, suggested in a recent speech that the more aggressive a corporation's treasury management practices are, the more responsibility that corporation has to ensure that its banks fully understand how it is operating its accounts.

One procedure on the list may have been misunderstood by a number of the respondents. Anticipatory drafting is often used for collecting of store receipts in the retail business and covered by agreement with the depository banks concerned. For example, the cash manager of a department store chain may cut a depository transfer check on Friday anticipating the Saturday receipts of the stores' depository banks.

Guidelines for Internal Cash Management Audit

Auditors have used a cash management procedures document in their periodic review in half of the corporations that responded. However, there is still concern that they need to learn more about float, bank products, and bank compensation. Auditors tend to focus more on accounting entries and less on the time value of money. In this light, Cassa Palmer, a vice president at the Philadelphia National Bank, has conducted all-day seminars to help auditors become more familiar with cash management. She recommends the following documentation to ensure a thorough, periodic audit of the cash management function:

1. *Cash management policy statement.* It should be formalized in writing and reviewed periodically by either the board of directors or senior management. It should conform with the business objectives of the corporation.
2. *Investment policy statement.* There are recommendations for such a policy in Chapter 3.
3. *Cash management procedures outline.* Each collection, concentration, investment, and disbursement procedure should be described step-by-step so that the auditors can easily understand and follow it. In writing and updating such a document, the treasurer or cash manager should treat it as a "thought piece" and reevaluate the basic business justification for each cash management practice.
4. *Letter to each bank.* Such a letter should document the company's cash management procedures. It should state that the company does not intend to overdraw its accounts or draw on uncollected funds except under unusual circumstances, such as money transfer or other errors, and intends to compensate fully the bank when overdrafts and uncollected funds do occur. In addition, Ms. Palmer recommends as a courtesy to the bank, a forewarning of unusual activity, such as a drawdown at the end of the quarter, to compensate for excess balances maintained.

Checklist for Auditors

The following items might be included on either an internal or external auditor's checklist:

1. Cash management policies and procedures should be reviewed by both internal and external auditors.
2. Primary personal responsibility for both policy and day-to-day implementation should be specifically defined. Secondary responsibility should be defined in the primary person's absence.
3. Policies and procedures should be frequently updated, especially given recent changes in available products and techniques.
4. Account analyses should be reviewed for adequacy of bank compensation. Fees should be reconciled with the services provided. Bank and internal records of transaction volume should be reconciled. Are the fees being levied at the right time? Are the prices in line with agreement between the bank and the company? Does the bank reflect overdrafts and uncollected positions accurately? How does the bank calculate its earnings credit rate?
5. Both book overdrafts and uncollected funds should be questioned. Is any arbitrage of funds taking place?

6. Concentration of funds should be reviewed for possible chaining.
7. Money transfer procedures should be reviewed. Are there adequate safeguards, such as the requirement of two people, each with a personal, confidential code identifier number, and single transaction limits for telephone- and computer-terminal-initiated money transfers? Do the procedures for bank call-back work correctly? Are only repetitive transfers going from one of the corporation's accounts to another used in the computer system, or is there provision for "free-form" transfers to third parties as well? Who is authorized to execute the free-form transfers?
8. Under reverse "repo" agreements, who are the borrowers? Is the collateral adequate? How is it documented? Who is the agent, and who is the principal?
9. If the company has point-of-sale terminals, there should be written back-up procedures in the event the system goes down.

Summary and Conclusions

Significance of Hutton The abusive practices cited in the E. F. Hutton case were unusual and not representative of cash management in the corporate community at large. They bore a strong resemblance to check-kiting cases in the past; only the technology had changed. Unlike sophisticated corporations and banks, which might try to gain float from one another with widely used cash management practices, Hutton deceived its banks in the way it used its deposit accounts and took advantage of deficiencies in the banks' information systems.

Cash Management Legislation Aside from cash management practices already cited by the Justice Department and the SEC, and a few state laws, not very much legislation has developed as a result of the Hutton incident. Legislation in the immediate future on corporate cash management appears unlikely because there is no aggrieved group pressing for it.

Corporate Reaction Corporate reaction was generally quiet. The Hutton affair initiated useful discussions on which cash management practices fell within the boundary of ethics and the law, and which did not. It gave companies a good excuse to document policies and procedures and to make sure that their auditors understood them and reviewed them regularly.

Lessons Learned by the Banks The Hutton case has alerted banks to improve their account analyses, to monitor uncollected funds and overdrafts more closely, and to be more cognizant of their customers' activities.

Recommendation In order to stay within the ground rules of cash management, corporations should make their cash management practices known and ensure that they are not deceiving their banks, vendors, or customers. Verbal agreements are acceptable but more difficult to prove in event that legal disputes develop. Written agreements and letters of intent are recommended to avoid misunderstandings.

3 Consolidation and Evolution: How Practices and Priorities Are Changing

In the survey, corporations were asked how their practices and priorities were changing throughout the cash management function. Recent events, such as Hutton and the daylight overdraft limits, are best understood in the evolutionary context of banking, the payments system, and cash management practices.

Organization of the Cash Management Function

The Hutton incident has focused attention on organizational structure because decentralization and imprecise personal accountability for cash management procedures were two important aspects of the Hutton environment that allowed the questionable practices to develop. While the majority responding to our questionnaire report that their organizational structure has not changed within the last year, one-third replied that cash management has become more centralized, and only one firm reported that it has become more decentralized. Relatively autonomous divisions, or subsidiaries operating as autonomous companies, was the reason given for a decentralized cash management structure in most cases. Reasons for increased centralization include cost saving and efficiency measures, desire to allocate compensation equitably among all relationship banks, greater ability of a central office to pull in, and act on, information as a result of computerized balance-reporting services and treasury workstations, and desire to have greater control over procedures to prevent Hutton-type incidents from taking place.

The treasurer is responsible for cash management policies and procedures, and a cash management or banking relations specialist under the treasurer is responsible for day-to-day cash management operations in two-thirds of the companies that replied to the questionnaire. The assistant treasurer, at a level in between the treasurer and the specialist, is responsible for policy for 10% of the respondents and for day-to-day operations for 10%. The CFO or another senior executive tends to be more involved in companies with sales under $1 billion; in many of those companies, the CFO and treasurer positions are combined. Titles for the cash management or banking specialist include director, Cash Management Operations; manager, Finance and Banking; and Treasury Operations manager. In several companies, day-to-day cash management is the responsibility of an accounting manager.

Cash Management Objectives

Corporations were asked how the relative importance of their cash management objectives and measurement systems had changed during the last year. In general, cost reduction and efficiency have become more important cash management objectives during the last year. Minimizing bank fees and other external costs was considered more important by 60% of the respondents. Almost half mentioned using the most efficient cash management tools offered by leading cash management banks. Minimizing bank demand balances, minimizing collection float, minimizing the internal cost of running the cash management function and maximizing the return on excess cash were mentioned by 40%. About 20% of the respondents mentioned minimizing internal book balances and providing adequate balance compensation to the banks, and only 15% mentioned maximizing disbursement float. There were relatively few objectives defined as "less important." Ten percent indicated specifically that maximizing disbursement float has become less important. With lower interest rates, and the review of cash management practices in light of Hutton, there appears to be less concern with float and more concern with containing costs and making treasury operations more efficient.

Quantitative Measures of the Cash Management Function

Should cash management be measured as a profit center within the treasury function? In a poll conducted in early 1985 by Louis Harris Associates and Manufacturers Hanover Trust Company, 60% of treasury managers believed that treasury areas would eventually be restructured as profit centers, but very few had actually followed through with such a restructuring. In this FERF survey, less than 5% of the respondents reported that the cash management function was measured as a profit center now, and less than 5% reported that they were considering it in the future. One large multinational cash manager reported that profit center measurement was exactly what his company wanted to avoid, because it encouraged incidents such as Hutton and Marsh & McLennan. The Marsh & McLennan incident in 1984 involved a risky government securities investment strategy that had produced highly visible profits, and bonuses to the investment manager, but backfired with a reversal of interest rates. It is described in more detail in the section on investment policy.

Sixty percent of the respondents to our survey measure the performance of their cash management function by the average level of cash versus target (either on the corporate balance sheet or in the form of bank collected balances) and about half cite the return on invested cash and bank compensation versus target. One-third use days sales outstanding, and one-third use accounts receivable turnover.

Nonquantitative Measures

As the scope of the cash management function broadens within the corporation, nonquantitative measures are becoming more important. The overall quality of bank relationships was a nonquantitative measure of the cash management function cited by 90% of the respondents. The majority also measure investment strategy and risk analysis, conformance with accepted practices, use of state-of-the-art techniques, the quality of forecasts, and the quality of information to management. One-third evaluate the cash management function in its role as a barometer of company liquidity.

One-third of the respondents also measure the role of other departments in the performance of the cash management function. One measures customer receipts against projections of the credit department, as well as days sales outstanding compared with other companies in the industry. A large retailer with internal check-processing centers measures the time required to deposit those checks in the banks.

Bank Services and Relationships

The perceived importance of the bank in the future, the quality and innovation of noncredit services, pricing, responsiveness, and bank capital adequacy and overall creditworthiness have become more important criteria for evaluating principal banking relationships in the last year. Less than half of those surveyed mentioned credit extension, and less than a quarter mentioned the availability schedule, the international branch network, the evaluation of management, and investment banking capabilities. The latter two criteria might have ranked higher in a survey of CFOs. Less than 10% mentioned the correspondent bank network and the domestic branch network.

Our findings on bank evaluation were compared with those of Greenwich Associates in their *1985 Report to Executives on Cash Management Services.* Competitive pricing, specialist expertise, and the need for a bank in the region were considered by corporate financial officers to be more important reasons for selecting cash management banks than they had been in previous years. The majority still considered a long-term historical relationship, credit facilities, and operations quality to be important as well.

Pricing and Account Analysis

In years past, pricing for noncredit services was not so important an issue for the banks as it is today. Corporations maintained more generous balances. Banks provided operating services to help justify them. Unit costing and account analyses were not very accurate, and pricing was not very scientific. There was little intelligence on other banks' prices. Analysis charges (prices for services translated into balance requirements) were in some cases just standard margins over unit costs. As higher interest rates and cash management services motivated corporations to reduce their balances, banks began to improve and automate the item count and unit costing of their noncredit services. The Monetary Control Act of 1980 gave banks further impetus to improve their costing and either to price at a profit or consider dropping the service concerned. Despite a number of bankers' comments in the questionnaire that their own institution's account analysis could still use some improvement, for the banking industry as a whole, the account analysis appears to have become a more accurate record of all services provided. There is less slack in customer balances and consequently less willingness by the banks to make up for losses on one or more services elsewhere in the relationship.

Most of the respondents considered the majority of their banks to provide either very accurate or moderately accurate account analyses. The most frequent response was that 75% of the banks are very accurate and 25% are not very accurate. Some complain that a number of their banks do not complete and mail their account analyses so promptly as they should. Corporations were also concerned about the inconsistency of terms and format among their banks and the time it takes to compare the account analyses with each other. A number commented favorably on the NCCMA's efforts to develop a standard account analysis.

An NCCMA committee sponsored by 26 banks and 16 regional cash management associations has been compiling an inventory of corporate needs and working with the banks since 1984. A questionnaire mailed to 1800 corporations elicited more than 600 responses. While acknowledging that true standardization would be virtually impossible, especially given the variety of services provided, corporations indicated an interest in more consistent terminology and format. They were interested in more detailed descriptions and less combining of services in summary categories. Adjustment of average balances for tax payments, adjustment for previous months' activity, location on the statement of noninterest-bearing CDs, and the basis for calculating the earnings credit rate were four of many areas cited for inconsistent treatment by the banks. Accuracy, on the other hand, did not appear to be so great a problem. According to the survey, banks tend to redesign their account analyses every three years. The committee's objective was not to develop a rigid format but to have a prototype that reflected the needs of the corporate community and could be used by the banks as a guideline.

Banks and vendors have addressed the inconsistency problem by writing software to combine information from the various bank account analyses into a single report and to compare bank prices for each service. Treasury Strategies, a Chicago-based consulting firm specializing in cash management, offers an IBM-PC-based software package called Treasury 1 that allows the user to input information on each bank's analysis exactly as it is received. The program generates a consolidated report using the terminology and format selected by the user.

In addition to being more attuned to the market and aware of their costs, banks have become more flexible about fees and analysis charges in pricing noncredit services. Eighty percent of the corporate respondents report that 75 to 100% of their banks offer a choice between balances and fees. Forty percent prefer to compensate the banks with a combination of balances and fees; 25% prefer fees alone; and 20% prefer balances alone. Fifteen percent report that they like to have flexibility between one and the other. Some companies we interviewed like to benefit from balances that flow through the banking system in day-to-day operations and pay the remainder due to the banks in fees. Most corporations report that less than 25% of their banks continue to allow double counting—using some of the balances maintained to pay for both services and credit line availability—and that their banks' pricing for credit and noncredit services is becoming less bundled.

The Treasury Strategies Bank Price Index has been tracking the rise in prices that banks charge their corporate customers since 1980. The index consists of eight product components: lockbox, incoming wire transfers, outgoing wire transfers, account reconcilement, cash concentration, disbursement services, balance reporting and account maintenance. As shown by the charts in Exhibit 3, the index measures both fees and analysis charges and compares the prices of money center and regional banks. The composite fee index released in May 1986, reflecting changes for the year 1985, was 180 measured against a level of 100 for 1980. The analysis charge index was 370. The large increase in analysis charges has been caused by a reduction in earnings credit rates as well as an increase in underlying prices. Anthony J. Carfang, a principal at Treasury Strategies, cites average earnings credit rates of 7.28% for 1986 versus 13.64% in 1980. Regional bank prices were 70% of prices for comparable services at money center banks in 1980, declined to 62% in 1983, and rose to 75% in 1985. The price increase for 1985 was a modest 2.7% in comparison to 13.3% in 1984 and 18.3% in 1983. Carfang thinks that this tapering off is not only in line with lower inflation throughout the economy but also shows that the banks have improved their service costing and made the majority of the big price adjustments that were encouraged by the Monetary Control Act. The increase started to taper off in the money center banks last year, and the same pattern was observed in the regionals this year.

Exhibit 3

Treasury Straegies Bank Price Index

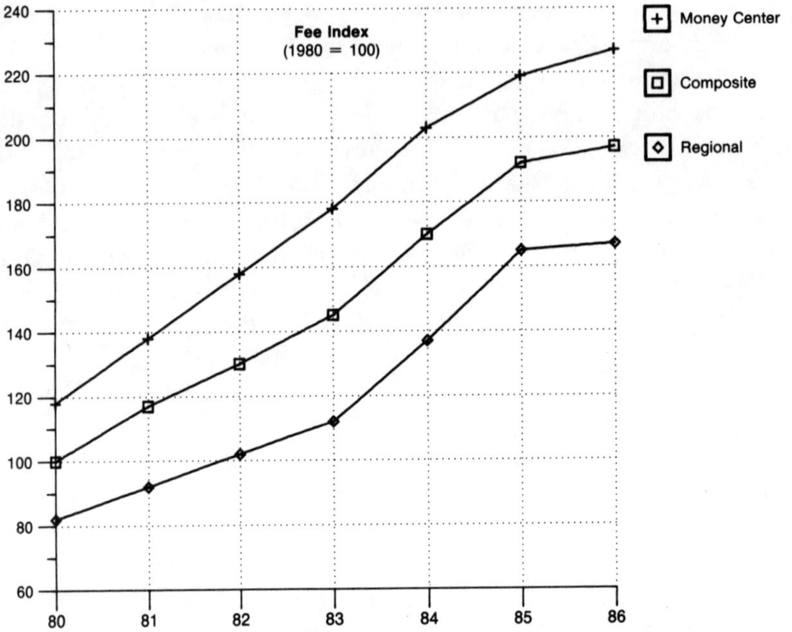

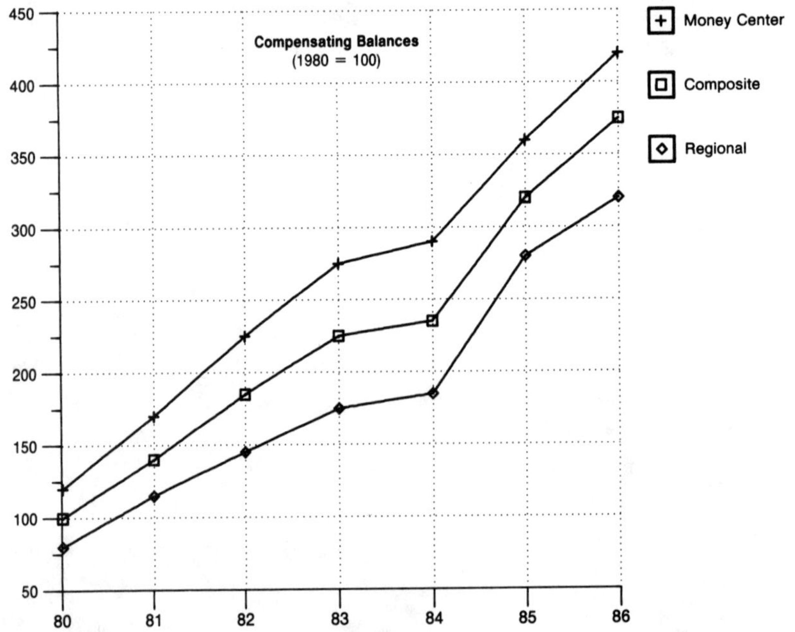

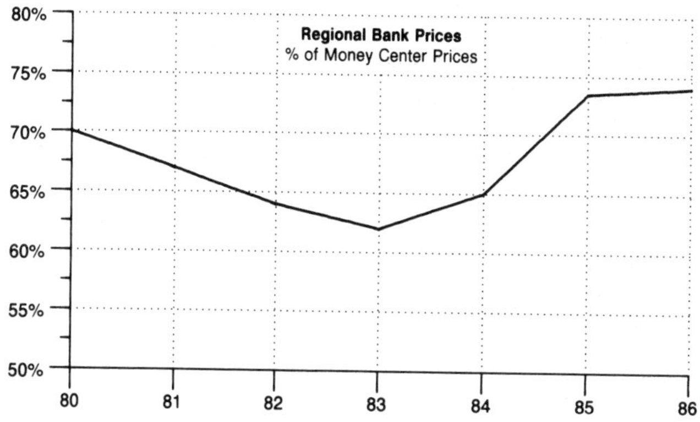

Of the 53 banks replying to our survey, 27 said that they offer customers a choice between fees and analysis charges for all of their noncredit services, 23 offer a choice for most services, and 3 offer it for just some services. Thirty-eight base their prices on what they perceive to be the market, but with unit costs taken into account. Eleven set their prices at a margin over fully absorbed cost, and two set them at a margin over direct cost. Forty-one prefer balances, and 12 prefer fees. Twenty believe that their pricing encourages the type of compensation they prefer, and 32 believe that it does not. Twenty-four of the 53 say that they offer some double counting between balances required for credit and noncredit services on a case-by-case basis. Double counting appears to still be more alive in the bankers' than in the corporations' perception.

Jack M. Meckler, senior vice president, First Wachovia Corporate Services, suggests a number of ways the corporation can keep bank costs under control:

— Consolidate banking relationships by reviewing the number of lockbox and disbursement banks, and using only one concentration bank. For example, by reducing its number of lockboxes, a corporation can save more in fees than it forgoes in float benefits.

— Reduce unnecessary operating services. A simple example might be eliminating extra photocopies from a bank lockbox that are no longer needed because of a new accounts receivable system.

— Reduce concentration costs by using the ACH instead of DTCs and money transfers and consider reducing the frequency of concentration payments. For example, if a retailer calculates the daily amount of receipts from a store, the rate paid in a local bank's money market account, and the cost of a transfer, once or twice each week might be the most economical frequency for concentration payments.

— Consider the feasibility of preauthorized payments for collection and compare costs of bank lockboxes and in-house processing.

— Negotiate price breaks for volume.

— For high-volume check deposits, negotiate possible cost savings and availability improvement from MICR-encoding and in-house separation by drawee bank.

— Ensure that differences in earnings allowances are taken into account in comparing bank prices. For example, banks differ in the way they adjust for reserve requirements and the way they adjust annual to monthly rates.

Negotiation of Availability

Large banks normally have schedules of their own availability for checks presented to each location in the country. Those schedules are based on standard check-clearing times and "direct-send" arrangements they make with other banks to improve on the availability offered by the Fed. Direct-send arrangements involve using courier services to present checks to other banks when the check volume is high enough to justify the cost. Banks may offer their customers availability for checks collected based strictly on the banks' own availability schedules, but they have developed other alternatives as well. They have negotiated overall float times based on individual analyses of customer check activity, and they have provided schedules of availability that might or might not coincide with the exact availability they are receiving—much as prices might vary from costs depending on the product, competition, and marketing objectives.

Although half of our respondents report that they have negotiated an availability schedule or an overall float factor for total availability, the majority at least perceive that the availability they are offered is according to the bank's availability schedule.

Product Management Trends in Banking

Meckler of First Wachovia cites several current trends in the banks' development of cash management and other noncredit services. Most corporations have been familiar with the basic banking services related to cash management for quite some time. The banks' cash management consulting activities are changing with the corporate cash management function and becoming broader and more concerned with the entire time line of cash management. New products today tend to require a substantial investment in systems—both hardware and software. As a result, product development time is longer, and earnings projections to justify the investments must be more rigorous. Fewer products can be developed by simply starting with a pilot project for one customer and offering the services to others if the pilot is successful. Meckler also cites the cash management press, which did not exist a few years ago. Articles bring our attention to what is new and what might happen in the near future. As a result, we might expect some developments to occur sooner than they actually will. ACH corporate trade payments might be an example.

Robert W. Quinlan, a vice president in charge of cash management services at Equitable Bank in Baltimore, cites the trend toward knowing what the customer wants but making sure the service is profitable and not just offering it because other banks are. More banks are becoming niche players, promoting the services in which they have a competitive advantage and dropping others that are not profitable.

Banks' Evaluation of Their Own Product Management Capabilities

With the self-evaluation and daylight overdraft cap program, bankers have had some good practice in self-rating this year. We took advantage of those skills with our survey. We asked them whether some of their own product management functions were good, or needed improvement. The majority thought that improvement was needed in the accuracy of unit costing, sales training for their relationship managers, and customer market research. Eighty-five percent rated the accuracy of their volume count as good, and the majority rated creativity in developing new products, sales training for specialists, and competitive intelligence on pricing as good. Except for the accuracy of volume count, the responses were not heavily weighted in one direction or the other. Thirty-two of the 53 bankers rate their own bank's measure of individual customer profitability as somewhat accurate, 13 rate it as very accurate, and 8 rate it not very accurate.

Information Reporting

Computerized balance and transaction reporting, and automatic retrieval with a treasury workstation have become virtually standard practice in large corporations. Half of our respondents report that they get real-time (intraday) balance and transaction information from at least a small number of their banks. About 20% are getting real-time information from 75% or more of their banks. The interest in real-time information varies with the corporation and type of transaction. Large customer payments with accompanying invoice detail, for example, are important for credit managers.

Almost half of the respondents reported some difficulty during the last year in having a bank report either directly to their computers or through another bank. Refusal to report at all is unusual now that balance reporting is so widespread. One large corporation reported difficulty in getting information consistently by 8:30 A.M. in New York from some of its East Coast money center banks.

Treasury Workstations

The introduction of the IBM PC and compatible machines gave the treasurer's office more convenient and less expensive access to computers than in the past. A strong demand for software developed, and both banks and specialized software firms responded to the new product opportunity.

Forty percent of our respondents retrieve balance and transaction information automatically from 75 to 100% of their banks with a treasury workstation. Sixty percent of the Greenwich respondents use a treasury workstation to prepare their cash worksheets, and more than 40% use it for developing consolidated bank balances, evaluating their target bank balance levels, and projecting cash balances.

The treasury workstation software offered today by most bank and nonbank vendors falls mostly into the category of information retrieval and management. Commonly offered functions include:

— *Bank balance and transaction retrieval.* Automatic retrieval of balance and transaction information from all banks and consolidation into one report.

— *Money transfer initiation.* Repetitive money transfers in which the debit and credit accounts are predefined by the corporate user are the most common for security reasons. Nonrepetitive options are usually available as well. Software normally allows the user to install several levels of password security in carrying out transfer instructions.

— *Target balance monitoring.* Tracking actual and target balances with each bank on a monthly and year-to-date basis.

— *Bank relationship management.* Basic reference information, such as account numbers, bank contacts and telephone numbers, resolutions, authorized signers, and signing limits.

- *Cash worksheet.* A worksheet that pulls information from other bank information reporting modules to fill in the previous close-of-day balances reported by each bank, all the different categories of debits and credits as that information is received, interim and projected net cash positions during the course of the day, and the end-of-day cash position. The customized credit columns on the worksheet might include lockbox receipts, corporate deposits, investments maturing that day, interest income, bank borrowings, and incoming money transfers. The debit columns might include amounts required to fund controlled disbursement accounts, outgoing wire transfers, loan repayments, interest payments, and investments to be settled that day.
- *Plan/actual forecast sheets.* Allowing comparison of actual numbers with plans and constant revision of forecasts.
- *Reconciliation.* Comparing bank transactions with company-initiated transactions.
- *General ledger entries.* Communicated in the correct format for the mainframe accounting system.
- *Trade services.* Initiation of letters of credit and amendments; status reports on letters of credit, documentary collections, and bankers' acceptances.

Personal computers are becoming more powerful every day. Today's largest PCs have the capacity of yesterday's mainframes, and software is developing at the same pace. Treasury workstations will soon go beyond information retrieval and management. Some of the developments in treasury workstations we might see in the near future include:

- *More coordination between the micro and other systems.* The treasury function's use of the microcomputer has almost outgrown the microcomputer. Some data bases, such as the corporate accounts receivable and payable ledgers, will be too large to store on a microcomputer. Some information will be stored on the mainframe for audit trail purposes.
- *Expert systems.* Software will go beyond collecting and organizing information. For example, it might be able to search the substantial commercial and investment bank databases that already exist and design optimum investment portfolios based on instrument, credit rating, maturity, issuer limit, and other criteria. Such functions as money transfers for concentration or other payments within the corporate network might be automated based on target balance levels, for example.
- *Bank investigations.* Software might be written to inquire about errors in bank transactions.

- *Intraday cash management.* There will be greater availability of real-time information, allowing the initiation of more bank transactions by computer during the day. Certain defined transactions, such as large incoming money transfers, might be automatically transmitted by the bank and trigger a signal to the corporate user.
- *Working capital management.* As we see the cash management function broaden in scope to include working capital management, the integration of the treasury workstation with the mainframe and other systems and the interdivisional sharing of information might enable the cash manager to pull together all of the information he or she needs for total working capital forecasting and management.

The banks played a strong role in 1982 and 1983 in introducing treasury workstations to the corporate marketplace. However, a number have recently retreated from developing and offering products in this area—particularly software options that do not relate directly to bank transaction information and initiation. After selling their treasury workstations, banks have had to make highly qualified people available for customer support. For example, the majority of the Greenwich respondents expect banks that provide treasury workstations to provide consulting, data files, and other support services. For most banks, the total market is not large enough to justify the expense of customer support. Furthermore, a number of large corporations prefer to program applications suited to their own particular needs internally and are generally not receptive to generic bank products unless they are directly related to bank information retrieval and transaction initiation.

Collection

Collection methods have not changed very much in the last three years, according to our respondents. Checks mailed to lockboxes and wire transfers are each used more by half of the respondents. A quarter of those surveyed cite increased use of preauthorized ACH debits; they were from a variety of industries, including processing, consumer goods, hospital and health care, and other financial services. Even after the many years that lockboxes have been used as a collection method, 40% cited increased use of lockboxes, and 25% cited less collection by means of checks mailed to the office. Five of the six retailers that responded cite increased use of credit cards.

Half of our respondents expect to collect some or all of their trade payments through the ACH or a similar electronic means in the future. Of those that do not opt for that method, half believe that payers will resist because of float loss or administrative reasons, and half would not want to make the switch until ACH trade payments became standard industry practice. One large consumer products company has negotiated an adjustment of payment terms with its largest vendors to encourage ACH payments.

Eighty-five percent of the respondents have lockboxes, and 55% of those lockbox users designed their lockbox systems in house, negotiating with banks individually. Forty percent used a bank consultant, and only three of the respondents used a private consultant. Forty-five percent has selected from one to five banks independently for their lockbox services. Fifteen percent has selected from 6 to 10 banks independently, and 25% has selected more than 10 banks independently.

Of the 171 lockbox users, 15 use a coordinated lockbox system consisting of several banks, and three use one bank's nationwide lockbox system. Half of those using a coordinated system and the three using one bank's nationwide system had sales of less than $1 billion. Some of the large corporations we interviewed expressed reservation about the primary lockbox bank's ability to control other banks in a lockbox network. Some cited the ability to get better prices when negotiating with each bank independently, often taking other credit and noncredit services into account as well. Some of the banks developing their own nationwide networks are reportedly having a problem maintaining sufficient volume to retain an independent ZIP code, an important mail time factor. However, the lockbox networks appear to be a good service for middle-market corporations that have sufficient sales volume throughout the country to justify several lockbox collection points but do not have other reasons to justify the expense of establishing additional banking relationships in other regions.

Bank lockboxes are not for everyone. One large manufacturer collects checks in sales offices throughout the country and immediately updates a centralized accounts receivable file. A large retailer is able to process more economically with an internal system and points out that with smaller consumer payments, per-item processing cost is more important than float.

The new imaging technologies used by the leading lockbox banks, designed for their own processing speed and cost saving, have just begun to improve service in their customers' perception. Operating quality temporarily declined in some banks while converting to the new equipment.

The regional banks that have made a specialty of lockbox and other cash management services tend to get high marks from the large corporations with nationwide lockbox networks. Their costs are lower than corporations in larger cities, and in the words of one manager of cash management and banking, "They do what they do extremely well."

Fifty-five percent of the respondents report that they have compared actual lockbox performance against the mail times that were used as the basis of their original lockbox selection. In a recent presentation, H. D. "Buddy" LeTourneau, senior vice president of North Carolina National Bank, and Gail Fitzpatrick, vice president of Bank of America, provided some guidelines on how to make such an evaluation:

1. Actual collection time can be calculated from information on the banks' account analyses. Multiply average float by the number of calendar days in the month to get total float for the month. Divide by total deposits for average calendar-day collection time for checks deposited. Adjust if necessary for other transactions, such as same-day-value money transfers.
2. Three types of float must be measured: mail float, bank processing float, and check collection (or availability) float.
3. In evaluating bank availability schedules, the corporation should pay particular attention to the cities where its highest volumes and dollar amounts of customer checks are drawn and to the deposit schedules followed by the respective banks.
4. Not all customers get the bank's best availability schedule; it must be negotiated.
5. Banks can provide periodic reports of actual availability, check-by-check, which the customer can evaluate in the context of the respective banks' availability schedules.
6. Mail times vary by bank within each city, depending on each bank's pick-up schedule.
7. Banks' end-of-business-day cutoff times, the times when they switch to next-calendar-day credit for checks deposited, vary considerably. A bank with a very early cutoff, such as 2:00 P.M. will show shorter check collection time because, for example, items entered into the clearing system this afternoon will be measured from tomorrow. However, those banks will also show longer mail or processing float.
8. Time lags between when an item is processed in the lockbox area and when it is deposited vary by bank. Some banks make deposits

more frequently than others. Availability schedules are realized only if critical deposit deadlines are met.

9. Deposit times and frequencies may vary depending on the adequacy of bank staffing during critical hours of the day, such as the very early morning hours when heavy mail volume is received.
10. A corporation doing the analysis described in steps 1–9 should be aware of the assumptions in the widely accepted University Analytics "Duke" lockbox model. Those assumptions do not always coincide with the service the customer will get from a particular bank. For example, the model assumes four deposits per day and weekend deposits. It assumes that the availability schedule in the model will be applied to all customers and that all mail retrieved two hours before each critical availability schedule deadline will be processed and deposited in time to meet that deadline.

In summary, the customer should know the limitations of the commonly used models for lockbox comparison and be aware of the information that banks are able to provide on actual availability. There is no substitute for an on-site audit of the bank's lockbox operation for the corporate user to assess how well the bank is adhering to such performance standards as turnaround time in processing incoming mail and frequency of deposits. Negotiation appears to be required if the customer wishes to receive the bank's best service.

Disbursement

Although state laws have been enacted recently that prohibit brokers from issuing checks to retail customers from out-of-state banks, disbursement practices were not at the core of the Hutton case. Nonetheless, the Hutton issue encouraged corporations to reevaluate all of their cash management practices, and corporations remembered the Fed's earlier concern over remote disbursing.

Although the majority of companies surveyed have not changed their disbursement procedures during the last three years, 30% have increased the use of ACH, and 25% have increased the use of money transfers. Those using the ACH more include 6 of 9 respondents in the insurance industry, 3 of 6 in retailing, and 14 of 29 in the processing industries.

Three-fourths of all respondents are using controlled disbursing. Half of those users report that they have questioned whether one of their existing or proposed controlled disbursing locations could be construed as remote disbursing locations. Some corporations have expressed reluctance to move their controlled disbursing to smaller cities than they are currently using. One energy company was already considering the discontinuance of two disbursement locations because it had cut back its retailing in those regions. Discussions that followed the Hutton incident helped confirm the decision. Thirty-five percent overall and 45% of those with sales over $1 billion have done mail time studies of check disbursement points within the last three years, and 15% did studies more than three years ago. Of the total who have done studies, 40% report that they have reevaluated those locations for possible implications of float extension in the last year.

However, Larry Marks, president of Phoenix-Hecht reports a fivefold increase in bank requests for disbursement studies on behalf of their corporate-consulting customers within the last year. He cites two reasons. First, the corporate cash manager wants to make sure he or she is realizing all of the benefits of controlled disbursing. Second, check clearing and mail times are expected to be stable enough in the foreseeable future to make a study worthwhile. That has not been the case during the last several years as the Fed has strived to eliminate float from the system. Now, the Fed has accomplished a large part of its objective; float was reduced from $6.7 billion in 1980 to $400 million in 1985. The average clearing time for the 10 slowest cities measured by Phoenix–Hecht declined from 3.48 to 2.48 days between March 1981 and January 1985. Helena, Montana, formerly a well-known remote disbursing site, declined from 3.79 to 2.38 days during that period. As a result, fewer sites are likely to be considered remote disbursing sites.

The banks and corporations have adapted to later check presentments and the high-dollar group sort with the help of the Fed's payor services, which notify the banks electronically of the checks that will be presented later in the day. Forty percent of the respondents using controlled disbursing are notified of final check presentment by their banks by 10:00 A.M., and 90% is notified by noon.

Money transfers are used predominantly for funding disbursement accounts. Thirty percent mentioned depository transfer checks, and 30% mentioned the ACH for funding those accounts.

Forty percent plan to use the ACH or a similar method for disbursements in the future, 25% do not plan to, and 35% are uncertain at this point in time. Those planning to adopt such a disbursement method are about evenly split among small dollar items—payments to individuals, large dollar items (trade payments), and all items. Those not planning to disburse through the ACH usually have quantifiable float benefits from their current check disbursement systems that they do not want to give up. Sixty percent of the NCCMA respondents indicated that they would make greater use of electronic payments systems if there were no float benefits from paper-based payments systems. In discussing his controlled disbursement system, one large corporate cash manager expressed continued amazement at the number of checks that "just sit out there" from companies that "still don't play the cash management game." A few also expected that they would incur internal administrative resistance if they switched to disbursing through the ACH, or expected that their customers would resist for administrative reasons despite collection float benefits. In addition to float costs, the NCCMA respondents cited operating costs, lack of format standardization, and the effort required to negotiate new credit terms as important factors preventing them from moving to electronic payments.

Electronic Corporate Trade Payments: Is ACH the Right Vehicle?

The checkless and cashless society first envisioned in the 1960s has not arrived. Electronic payment and transaction volume was less than 0.5% of all payments made in 1983. As confirmed by the Greenwich and the NCCMA reports, the direct deposit of employee payroll and concentration from regional banks, lockboxes, and retail locations have been the most popular applications of the ACH to date.

However, there is a growing belief among corporations and banks that electronic corporate trade payments will come into widespread use. The Yankee Group, a research firm in the field of new technology developments, predicts that one-third of the business transactions in the United States will be settled electronically by 1995. Corporations could benefit substantially from using the ACH or a similar electronic network for corporate trade payments. Automating the entire order-taking, billing, and collection cycle could yield substantial savings by reducing manhours and paperwork. With lower interest rates and the Fed's efforts to eliminate float from the system, float is becoming a weaker argument for maintaining paper-based payments systems.

There are two problems. First, until virtually everyone adopts such a system for collections and disbursements, those that use the electronic system will have to maintain their paper-based systems at the same time.

Second, the Fed and a number of large corporations believe that the ACH system, as currently configured, does not have the encryption and other security features that a large dollar payments system should have. A payment must go through many steps—payor to bank, to first ACH, (sometimes to second ACH), to second bank, to payee. In the words of one cash manager, "That's okay if everything works perfectly." Another disparages informal operating procedures, such as "throwing those tapes on a truck."

There have also reportedly been occasional operating problems with ACH payments. Some say those errors are caused by the system itself and claim that they are just normal operating errors made by bank personnel. At each step, tampering is a possibility and there is no mechanism to signal that tampering has taken place. Furthermore, there has been some dissatisfaction with NACHA's "CTP" corporate trade payments information transmission format. When descriptive information accompanying the payment, such as invoice numbers and discounts taken, reaches the payee's bank, it must still be conveyed by some other means to the payee. This partially defeats the purpose of electronic payments.

Fourteen thousand banks have some ACH payment and receipt volume today. Most of that relates to consumer payments, such as payroll and Social Security. Some large corporations believe that for electronic corporate trade payments to grow significantly, a separate parallel network operating through a smaller number of banks with a commitment to wholesale business would be required. On the other hand, the information transmission, encryption, and other security features required for an ideal corporate trade payments network could be expensive to develop and thus nullify some of the cost benefits of today's ACH.

Industry-Specific Payment Systems

Two examples of industry-specific systems are PetroClear and the Travel Agency Clearing System. PetroClear is a monthly netting system operated by eight major oil companies that regularly buy and sell petroleum products from each other. The system can save transportation expenses when one company has needs and the other has extra supplies in a given region. The twentieth of each month is known as "crude oil trade day." During the preceding few days, the sales and accounting functions of the eight companies work with each other to determine which of the invoices due through the twentieth of that month will be included in the current settlement. Letters are sent to document the agreements made. Each company either pays or receives one net amount through MBank in

Houston. The payment is made on the earliest day between the twenty-third and the twenty-seventh of the month that does not fall between Friday and Monday.

The Travel Agency Clearing System collects payments due from 27,000 travel agencies and remits the amounts due to 160 airlines once each week. Reports of payments to be made are submitted 10 days ahead of time. The actual payments on the weekly settlement date may be by money transfer, check, or direct debit. Six regional settlement banks and two data processing centers are involved. The system is popular with the airlines because it provides far prompter payment than billing the travel agents. There are other industries, such as chemicals, that reportedly have not been able to agree on settlement dates and other operating specifications and do not yet have netting systems.

Electronic Business Data Interchange: The ANSI X12 Standards

In 1978, the National Association of Credit Management's Credit Research Foundation asked the American National Standards Institute (ANSI) to develop a national cross-industry standard to electronic business data interchange (EBDI).[7] ANSI in turn accredited a committee known as X12 and approved a set of preliminary standards developed by that committee in 1983.

The ANSI X12 Business Data Interchange Standards consist of transaction set standards, a data dictionary, and transmission control standards. The transaction set standards define the format and content for specific business transaction documents. There are formats for documents including purchase orders, invoices, remittance/payment advices, purchase order acknowledgments, requests for price quotes, replies to quote requests, shipping notices, receiving advices, catalogs with prices, purchase order change requests, and purchase order change acknowledgments. The data dictionary defines the precise content for data elements used in building transaction sets. The transmission control standards define format requirements for the commonly used packet-switching networks.

[7] ANSI is a voluntary organization of 8000 public and private organizations dedicated to developing consistent standards in all areas through the consensus process.

Jack Shaw, head of the Atlanta-based consulting firm Electronic Cash Management, Inc., and a member of the X12 Committee, sees a number of advantages for corporations that implement standardized EBDI. They include increased accuracy and speed in purchasing and filling customer orders; better forecasting of sales, purchases, and inventory requirements; a resulting decrease in excess inventory requirements; and increased generation of working capital. Shaw sees EBDI as essential for the implementation of "just-in-time" manufacturing.

The EBDI movement will be helped considerably if the Automotive Industry Action Group carries out a pilot project that is reportedly in the planning stage. Some members claim that today's manual procedures result in errors in 5% of the documents generated and that the implementation of EBDI could save automobile companies a remarkable $200 per car. The group includes members from the major industries that supply the car manufacturers—steel, glass, rubber, textiles, and chemicals.

The real savings from EBDI would come from implementation throughout the corporation and avoiding duplicate paperwork throughout the order-taking and fulfillment, billing, and collection process. But standardization of the EBDI format is the first step. When the formats are fixed, corporations will feel more confident that the internal systems they design will be consistent with their vendors and suppliers in the foreseeable future.

Concentration Procedures

Consistent with the very principle of concentration, corporations tend to use as few concentration banks as possible. This is supported by trends cited in this study, such as centralization of the cash management function, consolidation of banking relationships, and minimization of bank charges. Sixty-five percent of the respondents report that they use one principal concentration bank. Twenty percent report that they have more than one principal concentration bank. Some of the very large corporations have more than one principal concentration bank because of the sheer size of their activity. Fifteen percent report that they have regional concentration banks as well as a principal concentration bank. The reasons most often cited for more than one concentration bank were the delegation of cash management to divisions or subsidiaries, and regional or divisional separation of their cash management activities for accounting reasons. Two large insurance agencies cited requirements in two states that funds be comingled within those states before being remitted to the main corporate concentration account. A large retailer cited the geographic organization of its accounting operations, and a large computer manufacturer cited time zones. Another large corporation cited smaller banks without electronic ACH capabilities that could not remit in the same manner as its other banks to the main concentration bank. In most cases, the use of regional concentration banks has not delayed the timely transfer of funds into the corporation's principal concentration bank.

The concentration methods that have changed most in the last three years appear to be the increasing use of the ACH and money transfers initiated by the head office and the decreasing use of money transfers initiated in the field. This is explained by the trend toward centralization of treasury operations and the ability of the treasurer or cash manager to initiate money transfers by computer.

Hardee's, a fast food chain of 2700 restaurants in 41 states, provides a good example of how the concentration methods have evolved. In the late 1960s, each branch manager made a deposit at a local bank and mailed a copy of the deposit slip to the head office. The head office normally realized good value on those funds in 10 to 15 days. In the early 1970s, the company started to use the National Data Corporation deposit-reporting service. Branch managers used an 800 number to call NDC with the amount of their deposits, NDC telexed the amounts to the Hardee's concentration bank, and the concentration bank cut paper depository transfer checks (DTCs). The head office had good funds in three days. As with most time-sharing systems, the NDC charges were high.

According to Richard Richardson, director of Cash Management, Hardee's had a number of reasons for installing point-of-sale terminals, connected to its main computer, throughout the restaurant system. They included inventory control, payroll, and market surveys (keying in a customer profile, such as "yuppie," to match the menu items purchased while ringing up the sale). Now those POS terminals communicate total receipts for the day to the central computer; that information is relayed to the concentration bank; and the concentration bank initiates an ACH debit on each depository bank. The time required for concentration has been further reduced to one day.

Concentration through ACH – Efficiency versus Risk

Although the ACH is not used extensively for corporate trade payments, it is growing in popularity as a less expensive alternative to wire transfers for concentration payments. Payments are normally pulled in by the concentration bank as part of the normal night-cycle debit origination.

Acknowledging the efficiency of the ACH for concentration payments, Elliott C. McIntee, associate director of Bank Operations for the Federal Reserve Board of Governors, also points out some risks as well. The originating bank pulling in the ACH concentration payments is at risk if it passes on a payment and the paying bank later refuses that item. The paying bank is at risk if it decides to refuse the item but does not do so on time. With all ACH payments, the bank sending the payment is responsible for that payment even if the debit party fails. In the case of a return item, the Fed is at risk if the initiating (receiving) bank fails before the item is returned. In other words, the Fed has the responsibility in lieu of the failed payee bank to return the debit amount to the payor bank.

Investment

Interest rate, foreign exchange, commodity price volatility, deregulation, and the blurring of competitive boundaries between one type of financial institution and another are among the reasons for increased innovation in capital markets product development today. In their capacity as both borrowers and investors, large corporate treasurers are constantly being exposed to the newest instruments by investment bankers.

Despite the profusion of new instruments, our survey shows that most corporations remain conservative in their short-term investment vehicles. Commercial paper, repos, bank certificates of deposit, and Euro time deposits are the investment instruments used most often by the respondents, followed by Euro CDs, bankers acceptances and municipals, and other tax exempts. Euro commercial paper is growing in use but not yet widespread; money market funds, interest-bearing bank accounts, bank sweep accounts, and master notes were reported in smaller numbers. A number of companies report that they are net borrowers, and some subsidiaries report that investments are handled at the parent level.

Some respondents mentioned Eurobonds and newer investment vehicles, such as asset sales by commercial banks to corporations, dividend capture (investing in common stock just in time to receive a dividend), adjustable rate preferred, convertible adjustable preferred, and money market preferred stock. Preferred stock offers the corporate investor the advantage of an 85% tax exclusion for dividends paid by one corporation to another. At the same time, it has had the disadvantage of principal risk, particularly in a volatile interest rate environment.

Adjustable rate preferred stock was developed to address that problem in 1981. However, dividends rising and falling with interest rates were not quite enough to prevent price volatility. Some of the bank issues suffered principal erosion after the Continental Illinois crisis. Despite a formula that adjusts the dividends, other marketplace factors can change the investors' required rate of return and price.

Convertible adjustable preferred, introduced in 1983 by Morgan Stanley, gives the investor the right to convert to common after each three-month dividend announcement date, at a rate sufficient to preserve principal but with a maximum number of common shares defined. With this instrument, there was some concern that the 85% tax exclusion of the CAP dividends could be disallowed by the IRS because the conversion feature relieved the investor of any risk, so that the instrument was not really an equity investment.

Money market preferred was introduced by Shearson Lehman in 1984 and first issued for its own parent, American Express. A new rate is determined in an auction among the investors every 49 days. That is just over the minimum holding period of 45 days for the dividend exclusion and conveniently set so that it falls on the same day of the week each time. The lowest rate bid that will sell the entire issue is the rate received by all investors. If there are not enough bids to sell out the issue, the price reverts to a formula. The possibility that bidders will not subscribe to the entire issue on one of the auction dates creates some liquidity risk to the investor who wants to sell.

Other trends we have noticed are the use of outside investment management firms and options and futures to hedge equity portfolios. Those practices apply primarily to larger portfolios, which include some money invested for the medium term.

In the opinion of one corporate cash manager who has invested in relatively new instruments, such as convertible preferred and asset sales, extra time and effort is required to learn the new instruments, and particular effort is required to educate and obtain the concurrence of all levels of management concerned with investment policy.

Alan G. Seidner, who heads his own investment management and consulting firm in Pasadena, California, stresses the need for a corporate investment policy to ensure that the person who bears responsibility for making investments will know what management wants *before* unforeseen problems or mistakes occur. He particularly warns against any kind of speculation, such as trying to forecast interest rates or foreign exchange rates. Even the professional traders can be wrong, and it is not a productive game for corporate treasurers and cash managers.

Seidner suggests the following basic components for an investment policy:

1. *Broad goals.* For a large corporation, it is not uncommon for preservation of principal to be first, liquidity to be second, and yield to be third.
2. *Authority and responsibility.* Who sets policy? Who executes it? Who monitors? Should the board of directors be involved in setting policy? In approving it? Who should sit on the investment committee? CEO? CFO? VP Finance? Treasurer? Who is authorized to make the investments? Who substitutes when that person is out? Should someone outside the investment function serve in an auditing capacity?
3. *Authorized investment instruments.* Credit rating qualifiers might be included for each one, for example, AA rating by both Moody's and Standard & Poor's for corporate bonds.
4. *Requirements for diversification.* There may be limitations by type of instrument, by type of issuer—location or industry—by single issuer, and increasingly important in today's market, by guarantor.
5. *Maturity guidelines.* Both maximum and average or weighted-average maturities might be included. Long maturities have greater market risk than many corporations are willing to incur, particularly with the volatile interest rates of the last several years.
6. *Periodic reports and audits.* How often? Circulated to whom? Auditors might want to review the types of instruments, maturities, and credit ratings against the written policy and look for such danger signals as a high number of trades in relation to maturing instruments.

An investment loss in 1984 by Marsh & McLennan, the world's largest insurance agency, illustrates the danger of senior management not being fully aware of the investment instruments being used and their inherent risks. The company had large amounts to invest for the short term, including its own cash and amounts received from customers that were not yet remitted to underwriters. Investment managers were not authorized to hold large long-term government bond positions but without violating the letter of the rules, purchased bonds before the date they were issued on a "when-issued" basis. During a large part of 1983, prices for government bonds were rising, and the investment manager could realize substantial profits immediately by selling the bonds when they were issued or later if the bonds were taken into the portfolio. This worked beautifully during the last quarter of 1983, when prices were rising. Leveraged by purchases on margin, the returns were reportedly 17% in comparison with 11 to 12% available for safer short-term investments. Cash management was treated as a profit center, and the investment manager concerned was rewarded with substantial bonuses. When prices declined in the first quarter of 1984, the strategy did not work so well. The investment manager was faced with the dilemma of taking immediate losses when the bonds were issued or holding them in portfolio in the hope that prices would rise again. The government bond portfolio peaked at $2 billion, and $165 million in pretax losses were incurred before any of the company's tracking systems brought the problem to senior management's attention.

Summary and Conclusions

Scope and Priorities of Corporate Cash Management E. F. Hutton, lower interest rates, and the concern with efficiency and productivity in all sectors of U.S. business have combined to change corporations' priorities and focus in cash management. Corporations that still benefit from float will sustain their check disbursement systems until they can identify hard dollar benefits from switching to other systems. But their creative energies and new projects are directed more toward efficiency and cost control. Bank consulting has followed the broader corporate definition of cash management and focused on the entire time line of cash management and the efficiency of all treasury operations.

Bank Product Development Refinements rather than startling new concepts have been the theme of recent bank product development. David Johns, executive vice president of Mellon Bank, describes it as evolution rather than revolution. Development of the customer's "window to the bank" still has a long way to go as banks include new services, more detailed and timely information on existing services, and more transactions that can be initiated by the customer using the computer terminal. Lockbox imaging technology and the on-line updating of customer account receivable files is just being refined and coming into wider use. At the same time, corporate users are learning the finer points of evaluating lockbox services; breaking float into its mail, processing, and clearing components; comparing promised with actual availability; and making on-site inspections to check on the timeliness of opening the mail, processing, and meeting deposit deadlines.

Banks are taking a harder look at spending the money for new products. New product development usually requires hardware and software and a substantial commitment of money and time. It is harder today to develop a new cash management product by trying a pilot project with one customer and simply offering it to others if it works.

The chain of events beginning with the Monetary Control Act of 1980, charges for Fed services, improved cost calculations, and more accurate account analyses has resulted in more concern to make each product profitable and less tolerance of products that are just clever new ideas.

Banks are more willing to give up products in which they do not have a sustainable competitive advantage. Even the largest banks are not willing to compete in all areas today. There are more niche competitors. This is consistent with the thrust of strategic planners' thinking in most of U.S. industry today.

Corporate Consolidation of Bank Relationships Corporations are consolidating the number of their banking relationships for reasons including cost reduction and bank creditworthiness. This does not mean that a corporation will expect one bank to provide all services. Excelling in a niche will be one of the ways to survive among a corporation's line banks, whether that be in the first, second, or third tier.

New Technologies New methods often do not come into common use so fast as available technology would allow them to. The ATM and the PC may be exceptions because of the speed with which they became part of our everyday lives, but corporate EFT and electronic business data interchange will have to overcome the momentum of established practice and quantifiable check disbursement float before they become common practice. How successful the automobile and related industries are in their pilot project may be an indicator of how fast EBDI will move. Integration of the treasury workstation with the mainframe and the development and application of electronic business data interchange development are trends that should support each other.

Investments A faster pace of product development in capital markets is bringing new instruments to the attention of the short-term corporate investor. Corporations are looking at new instruments receptively but carefully. Safety and liquidity tend to be ahead of yield in large corporations' investment criteria.

4 Daylight Overdraft Caps: Limiting Risk in the Payments System

Payments in the United States have grown far more rapidly than deposits or the gross national product in recent years. Most of that growth has been in large dollar transfers through the Fed Wire and CHIPS. Exhibit 4 shows that total payments for the year rose from $5 per dollar of GNP in 1950 to $65 in 1983. Exhibits 5 and 6 show the dollar and transaction volume growth in the Fed Wire and CHIPS systems.

EXHIBIT 4
Payments Compared to GNP

	Dollar Value of Payments ÷ Dollar Value of GNP	Dollar Value of Fed and CHIPS Wires ÷ Dollar Value of GNP
1950	5	1.8
1960	7	4.8
1970	16	12.6
1980	48	44.6
1983	65	61.8

Source: David B. Humphrey, Vice President Federal Reserve Bank of Richmond

EXHIBIT 5

Fed Wire Transaction and Dollar Volume

	Messages (millions)	Dollar Volume (trillions)
1978	29	50.5
1979	35	64.2
1980	43	78.6
1981	54	94.0
1982	58	121.2
1983	62	143.2
1984	68	158.7
1985	73	176.6

Source: Annual Reports of the Board of Governors of the Federal Reserve System

EXHIBIT 6

Chips Transaction and Dollar Volume

	Messages (millions)	Dollar Volume (trillions)
1978	9.6	20.4
1979	10.9	26.8
1980	13.2	37.1
1981	15.8	43.7
1982	18.6	53.0
1983	20.1	60.3
1984	22.8	69.1
1985	24.9	78.4

Source: New York Clearing House Association

According to figures compiled by Patricia Dowden, vice president at Philadelphia National Bank, $1.00 on deposit in the Federal Reserve System, which in accordance with bank reserve requirements corresponds to $8.00 in the commercial banking system, was matched by $1.50 in payments throughout the system in 1968. If only the money center banks were taken into account, that $1.00 at the Fed was matched by payments of $4.40. By 1984, payments had grown to $52 throughout the system and to $320 for the money center banks against each dollar at the Fed.

Today, about $1 trillion changes hands each day in the United States. By way of comparison, GNP is $4 trillion for the whole year. The daily total is broken down by payment system as follows:

	(approximate billions)
Fed Wire	$ 400
CHIPS	250
Government Securities Book Entry Account	200
Checks	150
Cash	0.1
ACH and Other	0.4

The Federal Reserve Bank of New York maintains the record of ownership of U.S. Government securities in book entry form. Money center banks act as securities clearing agents for the Fed, paying funds to the sellers and receiving funds from the buyers as those securities are traded and notifying the Fed of changes to be made in the book entry account. Payments for settlement are normally made the day after the trades take place.

Only 10 to 15% of the $1 trillion total is estimated to be for goods and services. What is the reason for this staggering increase in payments volume? The late 1970s and early 1980s were an unprecedented period of foreign exchange and interest rate volatility. The dollar rose to an unbelievable degree against other currencies from 1980 to 1985 as a result of the U.S. deficit, expectation of a larger deficit, record-setting interest rates, and the continued reputation of the United States as a safe haven for investments. Transactions between the dollar and other currencies grew accordingly. Short-term interest rates rose above 20% in 1980.

A new era of interest rate volatility began. No longer could borrowers and investors arrange long-term facilities and just leave them in place. A host of new financial instruments was developed to help them cope—swaps, options, caps, and collars, to name only a few. Each of these products resulted in new transactions. Financial institutions traded for their own position many times the amounts they traded on their customers' behalf. Government securities, once a safe and stable investment, became actively traded as prices moved with interest rates.

Reasons for Daylight Overdrafts

In the mid 1970s, the Fed became aware of a phenomenon known as *daylight overdrafts.* A daylight overdraft results from an excess of payments over receipts during the course of the working day that is normally expected to be reversed before the day is over. That overdraft might be in a customer's account in a bank, in a bank's reserve account at the Fed, or a bank's net position of payments and receipts over CHIPS. Today, about 170 banks processing daily payments of about $650 billion incur daylight overdrafts that average about $110 billion. Half of those daylight overdrafts are incurred by about two dozen banks. The $110 billion total is divided about evenly among the Fed Wire, CHIPS, and the government securities book entry account.

Some transactions in the money markets tend to create funds inflows for the banks in the morning and outflows in the afternoon; others are the other way around. For example, funds flow into a bank early in the morning from the return of Fed funds sold the night before, from the sale of government securities held for customers in custody, from check collections, and from incoming ACH payments. (At the beginning of the day, incoming ACH items are added to a bank's reserve account, and outgoing ACH items are subtracted for daylight overdraft tracking purposes.) Funds flow out of a bank from the return of Fed funds borrowed the night before, from the return of government securities to dealers, from checks presented to the bank for payment, and from outgoing ACH payments. Thus, a bank's pattern of daylight overdrafts is somewhat determined by its mix of business.

An important component in the volume of daylight is the Fed funds market, the most important vehicle through which banks lend to each other. Banks with excess funds in their reserve accounts at the Fed lend to other banks in need of funds simply by transferring funds from one reserve account to another. In 1981, Fed funds transactions were 44% of Fed Wire dollar volume.

It has been normal operating procedure for the bank lending funds to transfer those funds to the borrower at the end of the day and for the bank borrowing funds to return them first thing the next morning. Because of that procedure, a bank that is a consistent borrower of Fed funds does not have use of those funds between the time that it returns the borrowing for the previous night and the time it arranges a new borrowing for the upcoming night. Fed funds borrowings for more than one day, known as *term Fed funds*, are not used so often in bank funding because they are included in the lender's legal lending limit.

In commercial paper transactions, the borrower tends to receive funds late in the afternoon, after the issuing agent has created the note and received funds from the investor, and to return funds to the investor first thing in the morning. The bank inherently creates daylight overdrafts in its role as agent for the commercial paper issuer/borrower. A large portion of commercial paper investments are rolled over each day. The agent bank debits the commercial paper borrower's account in the morning, returns the funds to the investor, and then receives funds from the investor and credits the borrower late in the afternoon. The bank has the burden of the daylight overdraft during the interim period.

Most large foreign banks have substantial dollar transaction volume, including foreign exchange, letters of credit, documentary and check collections, and securities. Each bank tends to have a New York *clearing bank* to handle payments through CHIPS to settle those transactions. Clearing accounts run daylight overdrafts by their very nature. The foreign bank telexes payment instructions each day to its New York clearing bank, including also a list of payments that the clearing bank should expect to receive. Faced with heavy money transfer processing requirements each day, the clearing bank inputs or "stores" transactions in its automated money transfer systems (which communicates directly with CHIPS) as early as possible in the day. Instructions may be received from the customer and stored in the system on a previous day as well. Transfers are released automatically from the bank's money transfer system to the CHIPS computer starting at 7:30 A.M. By allowing payments to be made on a customer's behalf before payments for that customer are received from other banks, the clearing banks provide daylight overdraft accommodations. Each customer has a credit limit that is stored in the bank's money transfer system. That limit is overridden with only the approval of a credit officer. Theoretically, a "gridlock" could occur if a customer of Bank A reached his or her limit and the payments that were being held were needed by a customer in Bank B, who had also reached his or her limit, to make payments to a customer in Bank C, and so forth.

Benefits and Risks of Daylight Overdrafts

By allowing customers to incur daylight overdrafts, banks help commerce to function more quickly and efficiently. Banks have to process money transfers as early as possible in the day to cope with their volume. Banks and dealers assume that payments to settle foreign exchange trades and investment commitments will be made by the close of business on the normal settlement date. An active bank-clearing customer makes and receives a large number of settlement payments on a given day. It would be impossible for the bank to monitor all of those payments or to make each of those payments contingent on a receipt.

Today's payments systems create three kinds of risk for banks:

Sender risk is undertaken by a bank on behalf of the paying customer. If the bank makes a payment and thereby allows its customer to incur an overdraft, it runs the risk of not recovering funds from its customer.

Receiver risk is undertaken by a bank when it lets its receiving customer use funds before settlement. A bank participating in CHIPS may notify its customer of funds credited, and the customer may use those funds long before settlement at the end of the day.

Systemic risk is the risk that the failure of one major bank participant in such a system as CHIPS, and the subsequent cancellation of all of that participant's payments and receipts on the day of failure, could cause a chain of payment failures and liquidity shortages and drag down several other major banks in the process.

Transfers made through the Federal Reserve System by means of the Fed Wire can be treated as *final payments.* Receiving banks do not incur receiver risk in allowing the customers they credit to use the funds immediately.

Transfers made through CHIPS are provisional; they cannot be treated as final until the participating banks settle with each other at the end of the day. According to the CHIPS rules, banks have the right to recover payments from the customers that they have credited in the event of a bank failure scenario. However, the rights and liabilities in the event of such a scenario are not clearly spelled out and have not been tested. Participants in CHIPS lack both the protection and finality of Fed Wire transfers, wherein the Fed assumes the risk, and a mechanism for spreading the risk among all of the members, as the stock and commodity exchanges have. The Uniform Commercial Code does not cover electronic payments as well as it covers payments by check. An amendment to the UCC on electronic payments is currently being drafted by the Confererence of State Commissioners on Uniform State Laws.

The payments system creates risk for corporations as well. Take the example of one corporation, the payor, using a money transfer to discharge a trade obligation to another corporation, the payee. The payor instructs his or her bank, Bank A, to charge his or her account and pay Bank B for credit to the account of the payee. Bank A charges his or her account and remits through either the Fed Wire or CHIPS to Bank B. Bank B fails after the payor has legally discharged his or her obligation but before the payee has had the opportunity to withdraw the funds.

The Fed has been concerned about the risk of daylight overdrafts for more than 10 years. The Bank Herstatt and Franklin National Bank failures in 1974 caused bankers to think about the consequences of another bank failure. The Fed did not have the systems to measure daylight overdrafts until 1979 and even today, can monitor them on only an ex post facto basis. The window of risk for the participating banks was even wider before October 1981, when CHIPS shifted from next-morning to same-day settlement.

At the same time that the Fed was growing more concerned about daylight overdrafts, the banking industry started its own efforts to deal with that and other payments system issues. The Payments System Committee of the Association of Reserve City Bankers commissioned Arthur D. Little, Inc., and a committee of academic experts to conduct a comprehensive study of the nation's payments system.

Report on the Payments System, published in 1982, addressed a number of strategic issues related to technology, capacity, competition, regulation, and risk. The Bank Wire was still operating at that time, and the report noted that there was redundancy in the payments system. There was a need for a reevaluation of growth, capacity, and the system best suited to each type of payment. In banking and industry, there was a lack of total commitment to the use of the most efficient available payments system technology, such as check truncation, preauthorized payments, and debit cards.

Until 1980, commercial banks dominated the payments system because no other kind of institution could offer checking accounts. The Monetary Control Act changed their competitive position by allowing savings and loan associations to offer NOW accounts. At the same time, bank deposits began to flow into money market accounts and brokerage accounts with check-writing privileges. Banks had historically borne the cost and the risk of payment services in return for their franchise to hold demand deposits. Now money transfer volume was growing and deposits were declining. Credit, fraud, and operational risks related to the payments system were difficult to quantify. They were not covered by statutes, contracts, or insurance. There was a need for a payments system code to perform the role that the Uniform Commercial Code does for check transactions. Just as with the Hutton affair, the law had not caught up with technology.

Having identified risk as one of the major issues, the Payments System Committee convened the Risk Task Force. In October 1983, the Task Force published a report on the credit and fraud risks in the payments system and in 1984, published a report recommending a system of *voluntary ratings* and *daylight overdraft caps.* The committee worked closely with three officers of the Federal Reserve Board of Governors who served in an advisory capacity. By working closely with the Fed, members of the banking industry were able to develop a voluntary program to deal with the daylight overdraft risks and avert a mandatory program over which they would have less control.

The Voluntary Cap Program

The Large Dollar Payments System Advisory Group set the date of March 27, 1986 for the banks to begin a program of voluntary caps on their daylight overdrafts. Each bank defined a *net debit cap,* a limit on its total daylight overdrafts over all payments systems at any one time. Based on a voluntary self-rating system, the limit was defined as a multiple of bank capital (common stock, perpetual preferred stock, capital surplus, undivided profits, contingency reserves, and other capital reserves). Each bank also defined a *bilateral net credit limit,* the maximum amount of net payments that it was willing to receive *from each other bank* at any one time over each private network—CHIPS being the prime example.

Banks were asked to file their voluntary ratings with the Fed by the end of December 1985 and to have those voluntary ratings approved by their boards of directors by the end of February 1986. Any bank failing to do so would be prohibited from incurring any daylight overdrafts on the Fed Wire. Based on detailed guidelines published by the Fed and the Association of Reserve City Bankers, banks evaluated their creditworthiness, operational controls, and credit policies in comparison to peer groups. Within the category of creditworthiness, guidelines were developed for asset quality, capital, earnings, liquidity, and holding company strength. Every 15 minutes, for example, a bank with a top operational rating had to be able to monitor 95% of the dollar volume of all transactions, to calculate its net position across all wire systems, to compare that position with its daylight overdraft limit, and to monitor all significant customer debits and credits.

A bank's cap, the maximum daylight overdraft as a multiple of adjusted primary capital, is determined by the bank's rating under the voluntary self-assessment program. The maximum daylight overdraft for any single day and the maximum average for a two-week period fall into one of four categories.

Cap Class	*Two-Week Average*	*Single Day*
High	2.0	3.0
Above average	1.5	2.5
Average	1.0	1.5
No cap	0	0

Over 2200 institutions filed caps. They represented 43% of the banks that had incurred daylight overdrafts during a survey conducted by the Fed in December. Of those institutions, 13% filed for the highest cap; 30% filed for the above average cap; 37% filed for the average cap; and 20% filed for the lowest, no cap, category. The ratings were different among the 50 top overdrafting banks. Fifty-two percent filed for the high cap; 28% filed for the above average cap; 12% filed for the average cap; and 4% filed for no cap. The Fed expressed some dismay that so many of the heaviest overdrafting banks filed for the highest cap, but it also noted that the actual overdrafts for most of these banks were still reasonable in relation to their capital.

The caps for this first stage were deliberately set at a level that would not cause substantial problems for banks or corporations. The Fed recognized that the banks would need time to adjust to the program. They could start by looking for the easiest operational measures to reduce their daylight overdrafts.

As expected, March 27 was a nonevent. The payments gridlock that some feared when the program was first announced did not occur. A number of banks have kept their daylight overdraft position under control by limiting their customer's daylight overdrafts. Individual customer positions are being monitored closely during the day. Banks have purchased new money transfer systems that have customer-monitoring capabilities, as well as software to run on their existing money transfer systems.

Going forward, banks will be required to evaluate themselves twice each year and to have those ratings approved by their boards of directors. The Federal Reserve examiners will review the ratings. The Fed will see how successful the banks' daylight overdraft reduction efforts are. It may define tighter caps to be implemented in a year or so, corresponding to the banks' improved abilities to live within their caps. The Fed will collect data "ex post" to monitor each bank's position on both the Fed Wire and CHIPS at 15-minute intervals throughout the day. It will compile and analyze each bank's activity with a lag time from 10 days to 2 weeks. There will be tolerance for banks to exceed their limits on occasion. However, banks that do so frequently will be "invited to lunch" by the Fed to explain the reasons why and to outline the corrective measures they are taking.

Measures for Dealing with Tighter Caps

Although individual customer daylight overdraft limits seem sufficient for most banks to deal with the current daylight overdraft limits, a number of measures within the banking industry and individual banks are being proposed for the time when the limits become tighter. The industrywide measures would create rollover mechanisms for some of the transactions that inherently create daylight overdrafts and change the timing of others.

Commercial Paper Rollovers

A large portion of commercial paper investments made each day are in effect rollovers, but the documents and the funds must still move each time among the borrower, the investor, and the issuing agent. A group of Chicago banks is developing a rollover mechanism for commercial paper in which money transfers would not have to be made each time.

Fed Funds Timing

The American Bankers Association (A.B.A.) has developed new guidelines for the timing of Fed funds transactions. It expects them to be implemented by the summer of 1986. Lending banks will be encouraged to advance funds to borrowers within one hour of the time that loans are arranged. This in itself could substantially reduce daylight overdrafts because most

Fed funds trading takes place before 11:00 A.M. Borrowing banks will be encouraged to return funds to lending banks as early in the morning as possible but will be allowed to do so as late as noon.

Fed Funds Rollovers

The A.B.A. has also developed guidelines for rolling over Fed funds transactions and for increasing or decreasing Fed funds borrowings on a net basis. The Fed funds market is responsible for about one-third of the average day's $110 to 120 billion daylight overdraft, and about half of Fed funds borrowings are rolled over each day.

Intraday Fed Funds Market

There has also been some speculation within the banking industry that an intraday Fed funds market will develop. Some banks may lend portions of their daylight overdraft caps to other banks that need them. In so doing, a lending bank might increase its daylight overdraft by sending Fed funds to another bank, but presumably it would be staying within its cap. Such a practice could be criticized because the lending bank would be earning money on a resource—the daylight overdraft in its account at the Fed—that it was getting from the Fed without cost.

How well will these measures work, and how long will they take to implement? If reasonable progress can be shown in implementing these operational measures, the Fed may be persuaded to delay further tightening of the caps. At this point in time, the A.B.A. Fed funds trading guidelines have the best prospect for success, but it remains to be seen whether the banks' trading desks and money transfer departments will be able to comply with the guidelines in a consistent and timely manner.

The intraday Fed funds market raises both operational and pricing questions. Can funds be reliably advanced from lender to borrower and back again within such tight time frames? Will trading desks and money transfer departments have to develop a new category of high priority money transfers? Such a requirement could lead to a two-tiered system for all money transfers, a time-priority tier and a second tier that could arrive at the payee bank at any time before the end of the day.

How would intraday Fed funds be priced? Could hourly rates be developed? Would there be a rate for each intraday loan? The only precedent that comes close is the bank intraday broker loan. Rates start at about 100 basis points per day. Will the A.B.A. guidelines cause the beginning of the intraday Fed funds market? Under the new guidelines, there may be a substantial difference in pricing between Fed funds borrowed in the morning for return the next day by noon and funds borrowed in the afternoon. Funds borrowed in the morning would be, in effect, an overnight loan plus an intraday loan.

Bank and Corporate Views on Daylight Overdrafts

Banks were asked what measures they were considering to deal with daylight overdraft limits either this year or in the future if caps should be tightened. The percentages that are considering each of the measures are:

Netting Fed funds rollovers	42 %
Borrowing Fed funds for more than one day	42
Higher prices for priority money transfers	25
Individual-customer daylight overdraft limits	90
Charging customers for daylight overdrafts	38
Variable rate for overnight Fed funds depending on when customer agrees to return them	18
Surcharge for Fed funds not returned by the agreed time	23
Prioritizing transfers by customer	33
First come, first served for fully funded customers	33

Eighty percent of the corporations in the survey have had discussions concerning individual customer daylight overdraft limits. Forty percent have discussed higher priced priority transfers and the same percentage have discussed charges for daylight overdrafts. Sixty percent of the NCCMA respondents would like wire transfer services to remain open longer. Fifty-five percent would like to pay higher rates for time-of-day use of the wire transfer systems, and 55% would be willing to pay a premium to guarantee that a transaction would be completed within a set time frame, such as 15 minutes.

The banks were also asked what kinds of transactions they thought would be most affected if daylight overdraft limits were further tightened. Commercial paper issuance and investments, government securities investments in the secondary market, and other investment commitments were each mentioned by 40% of the respondents. Twenty-five percent mentioned payments within their corporate customer's networks, 20% mentioned payments between customers and suppliers, and 15% mentioned syndicate settlements.

For comparison, corporations were asked the same question. Eighty percent do not foresee any delays in their money transfers as a result of daylight overdraft limits. However, if delays did occur, 55% thought that they might affect commercial paper issuance and investments, 25% mentioned government securities investments in the secondary market, and 40% mentioned other investment commitments. Payments to and from suppliers and within the corporate network were each cited by 40%. Only five of the respondents mentioned syndicate settlements.

Eighty-five percent of the corporations indicated that they had discussed daylight overdrafts with their banks. Seventy percent have a good understanding of the daylight overdraft issue and how their own money transfer activity might or might not contribute to bank daylight overdrafts, while 10% know of the issue but are still confused about some aspects. Fifteen percent, including some with sales over $1 billion, are somewhat familiar, and 5%, all but one of those having sales below $1 billion, are not familiar with the daylight overdraft issue.

More than half of the respondents report that most of their banks have explained daylight overdrafts clearly. Thirty percent say that some have explained it clearly, but most have not. Fifteen percent, mainly with sales below $1 billion, report that most banks have not explained it clearly. Thirty-five percent report that either one or two, or several of the banks have discussed their self-assigned ratings used to determine the daylight overdraft caps. In the fall of 1985, shortly after the voluntary caps program was announced, there was speculation that the self-assigned ratings would be used by the stronger banks as competitive weapons, and the Fed then suggested that each bank keep its self-assigned rating confidential.

A quarter of the companies are considering some kind of netting to reduce their money transfer volume and thereby reduce their vulnerability to money transfer delays that might occur. Most of those considering netting acknowledge that some type of accounting procedures will have to be developed to substitute for banking statements and debit and credit advices as audit trails. By motivating netting, a technique that uses the exchange of information to reduce payment volume, daylight overdraft limits have encouraged corporations to think more about the potential for electronic business data interchange.

Half of the corporations specify routing, such as "through the Fed," in their money transfer instructions, and half only indicate the value dating, such as "same day value," that they want. Those that specify that transfers go through the Fed are either aware of the finality of Fed Wire transfers or are simply more familiar with the Fed as the mechanism for same day value transfers.

Forty percent of the bank respondents have talked to their corporate customers about the types of transactions that could cause daylight overdrafts and such measures as netting that could be used to guard against money transfer delays. Half of the banks would hold wires and half would continue processing when their daylight overdraft limit was reached. Those that would continue processing would presumably anticipate exceeding their daily limits on only isolated occasions and would plan to keep daylight overdrafts well within the lower two-week average limits. Two-thirds of the banks have set standards for the amount of time required to process money transfers after instructions are received. Those standards would protect a customer from reaching an individual daylight overdraft limit because of a bank's delay in crediting his or her account for an incoming money transfer.

Growing Importance of Bank Evaluation

Recent discussion of daylight overdraft limits and the voluntary cap program have focused corporate attention on bank risk and creditworthiness. As cited in Chapter 3, 109 of the 197 respondents report that creditworthiness and capital adequacy have become more important in the last year in their evaluation of banking relationships. Thirty-five of these respondents expect to reduce the number of their banking relationships as a result of the daylight overdraft issue.

During the last 15 years, large-bank loan losses, failures, and near failures have made credit analysis a two-way street between banks and corporations. Most of the large companies we interviewed do a regular bank analysis that includes tracking earnings, loan losses and reserves, liquidity, and capital in relation to both risk assets and total assets. Bank analysis services, such as those of Keefe, Bruyette and Woods, Cates Consulting Analysts, and Bank Valuation, have become increasingly visible to corporate treasurers and cash managers. With the accelerating pace of deregulation, competition, and new product development, banks have become more complex to analyze and more difficult to compare with one another. The banks themselves are aware of this, and one multinational commented on the improvement of information in bank annual reports and 10-Ks, particularly in the disclosure of off-balance-sheet exposures.

In the early 1970s, credit ratings for banks and bank holding companies did not exist, but a few institutional investors started to refuse to invest in nonrated bank holding company paper. Standard & Poor's and Moody's began to rate the banks, and the Securities and Exchange Commission developed comprehensive financial disclosure standards. Government-published machine-readable tapes became available; they disclosed financial information in far more detail than had been available to the public in bank financial statements.

In 1977, there were 12 banks rated AAA by Standard & Poor's; in 1985, there was only one. Crisis potential exists throughout the banking system. New York banks are holding Latin American debt that will be difficult to liquidate at face value. The reversal of oil prices has shaken banks in the Southwest that would have found it difficult not to participate in the boom mentality of the domestic energy build-up five years ago. On the other hand, the collapse of the Penn Square Bank in Oklahoma in 1982 exposed not only fraud and loans that should never have been made, but a lack of credit analysis and surveillance on the part of major New York and Chicago banks that participated in their loans. In the same year, the collapse of Drysdale, a New York government securities dealer, caused large loan losses in two major New York banks. A dealer borrowed securities to cover trading losses rather than just to support its inventory in the course of normal trading operations. A major bank lender sold securities to Drysdale under repurchase agreements that it had in turn purchased from other parties. The lender assumed incorrectly that it was acting only in an agent's capacity and that interest due to the other parties was the obligation of Drysdale. That turned out not to be the case. The Drysdale incident illustrated how a small, autonomous business unit of a large institution can become exposed to large risks and at least temporarily escape the notice of auditors, credit committees, and senior management.

There are a number of professional analysis services to help corporations track the health of their banks. Keefe, Bruyette & Woods has both credit and equity research staffs for bank analysis and acts as an underwriter and market maker for bank stocks as well. They provide their customers with a comparative rating service, periodic in-depth commentary, and access to analysts for questions. Their ratio analysis is augmented by frequent interviews with bank management. The annual

Keefe Bankbook details capital adequacy, earnings performance, and related measures in addition to underlying financial data for over 300 banks. It groups them geographically and ranks them by asset-size peer group. Ratios include:

Return on average total assets

Return on average earning assets

Return on average equity

Internal capital generation rate (net income minus dividends as a percentage of total equity)

Equity to asset ratio

Double-leverage ratio (parent company investment in subsidiaries plus parent company goodwill as a percentage of total parent company equity)

Year-end reserves, net charge-offs, and nonperforming assets as a percentage of total loans

Net interest margin

Dividend payout ratio

Cates Consulting Analysts and Bank Valuation rely on ratio analysis and prefer not to have their objectivity biased by interviews with bank management. David Cates runs a regular bank analysis course that his firm first developed for the Federal Deposit Insurance Corporation. He served as a consultant to Standard & Poor's in 1974 when they started to rate the banks. Cates emphasizes the interrelationship of ratios as predictors of bank failure. He sees seven "deadly" risks in banking:

1. *Asset quality risk*. Cates warns that loan charge-offs are rarely an advance signal of bank failure, because they are usually made too late. He looks for earlier signs of trouble, such as unusually rapid loan growth coupled with a decrease in margins.
2. *Funding risk*. This applies to banks that rely on uninsured funding. Market perception is of critical importance. If potential depositors believe there are problems in the loan portfolio, asset quality risk will become coupled with funding risk.
3. *Interest rate risk*. An example is the thrift industry, which experienced fixed-rate long-term earning assets and rising shorter term liabilities.
4. *Control risk*. Fraud is an example.
5. *Overhead risk*. A bank may take imprudent risks to compensate for escalating costs.

6. *Strategy risk.* A bank may adopt a strategy that is unrealistic or very expensive for the gains to be made. Examples are entering geographic markets that are already overcrowded with no particular competitive advantage or pursuing market share in such an area as large corporate lending at any price.
7. *Capital risk.* Cates considers the importance of capital adequacy to be overrated as a pure safety measure because banks are already too leveraged for that thin cushion to be of much help when there is trouble. However, it is important to the regulators, and a growing bank will have to raise capital in the future. Cates sees the banks' need to secure short-term funding and to raise capital as evidence of a healthy regulator at work—the market.

Although banks have been asked by the Fed not to reveal their caps, Cates suggests that corporations gather information to make their own judgment about whether there may be problems related to daylight overdrafts in the future. For example, they can ask the banks what their average daylight overdrafts have been in relation to primary capital.

Neil Reilly and Ray Gordon, managing directors of Bank Valuation, put particular emphasis on the asset side of liquidity. They reject one large bank's definition of liquidity, "continuous access to worldwide money markets," because it is too narrow. They agree with Cates that the liability side can fall apart if the asset quality and liquidity are there. Examples of ratios that Bank Valuation uses in its analysis are securities to total assets (loans are less liquid than securities); liquid, interest-bearing nonloan assets to total nonloan assets; and the premium or discount of the market value to the book value of securities. A bank holding securities at a premium will be more willing to sell them, booking a gain, than a bank holding securities at a discount, which would have to report a loss. The spread elasticity ratio is the ratio of interest income to interest expense. A ratio closer to one is a rough indication of more matched and less gapped funding.

All ratios have their limitations; for example, Gordon cautions that this last one does not indicate the degree to which a bank with a mismatched book is also hedged. Bank Valuation also estimates the adjusted liquidating value of the loan portfolio by analyzing six types of borrowers: domestic real estate, domestic agriculture, domestic commercial and industrial, domestic consumer, loans to domestic commercial banks, domestic loans for purchasing and carrying securities, and foreign loans. Because of the weight assigned to asset liquidity, the firm rates many of the regionals at the top of its risk profile of 50 banks, and many of the money center banks toward the bottom.

Summary and Conclusions

Capital Markets, Trading, and Transaction Volume At the same time that cash management is in a consolidation phase, the capital markets are undergoing rapid change motivated by the currency and interest rate volatilities of recent years, as well as by new competition among commercial and investment banks. Increased foreign exchange trading, government securities trading, swaps, futures, and options have all increased the banks' transaction volume.

Bank Intermediation While transaction volume has been increasing, the banks' deposit base has been eroding. Deregulation has allowed new nonbank competitors to pull deposits into money market funds and brokerage accounts with check-writing privileges. Corporations are funding through lower cost commercial paper. The uncontested franchise to keep free deposits compensated banks in the past for their costs and risks in acting as transactors. Now, all of that has changed. Higher transaction volume coupled with a lower deposit base means has created more risk for the banks, and a way to contain that risk or to compensate banks for it has not yet been developed.

Off-Balance-Sheet Risk Off-balance-sheet transactions, such as standby letters of credit and currency and interest rate swaps, are also increasing the perception of bank risk. The three bank regulatory bodies, the Federal Reserve Board of Governors, the Comptroller of the Currency, and the Federal Deposit Insurance Corporation, are all developing proposals for risk-adjusted capital requirements. The Financial Accounting Standards Board and several banks in their recent annual reports have addressed the issue of increased disclosure of off-balance-sheet risk.

Risk Reduction in the Payments System Setting the caps is just one step in the process of quantifying and controlling payments system risk. That concern started in the 1970s, and the problem will not be solved quickly. It is hard for either the banking industry or the Fed to define a safe level for daylight overdrafts or the level required to keep commerce moving. No method has been developed for achieving finality of payment on CHIPS or sharing the risk among the members.

New Payments System Conventions All of the easy ways to reduce daylight overdrafts are being implemented now. An additional lowering of the caps would require financial institutions to make some more difficult procedural changes. As these changes are explored, and efforts get underway to study daylight overdrafts related to government securities transactions, a whole new wave of product development related to book-entry securities transactions might begin. Global trading is a concurrent trend that may necessitate book-entry systems for all types of securities. The banks' daylight overdraft limitations may also support corporate and industrywide efforts to net money transfers, which could in turn support the electronic business data interchange movement.

Bank Consolidation The largest, best-capitalized, and geographically dispersed financial institutions will attempt to capitalize on the daylight overdraft issue by promoting the benefits of keeping transactions within one bank. Bank consolidation and interstate banking in the future could reduce problems relating to daylight overdrafts by increasing the number of transactions that take place within one financial institution.

Payments System Planning The Payments System Task Force noted in 1982 that there was some redundancy in the payments system and pointed out the need for an overall evaluation of each system and the kinds of transactions it was best suited to process. As the risk in the nonsettling CHIPS system is assessed, and corporations, banks, and the Fed debate whether the ACH is appropriate for corporate trade payments, there seems to be a continuing need for that type of planning. Ray McClintock of Mellon Bank points out, for example, that as banks' demand deposit accounting systems move more in the direction of real-time processing and the ACH moves toward a same-day capability, checks and the ACH will become a close substitute for the Fed Wire with its same-day, finality-of-payment feature.

Risk Assessment and Self-Regulation Responsibility for risk assessment and self-regulation is a theme that runs through both the Hutton issue as it pertains to corporate cash management practices and the daylight overdraft issue as it applies to the self-assigned ratings. The self-rating and daylight overdraft cap program is an important experiment for the banking industry in self-regulation, which if successful could be followed by other initiatives, such as an industry-sponsored effort to disclose off-balance-sheet activities more fully. With the banks, responsibility extends to the board of directors. They approve the ratings and could be held responsible if a bank failed partly because it had rated itself too highly.

5 Trends and Issues

What conclusions can be drawn concerning future directions of cash management and the payments system? What issues must be resolved?

Recent Changes

Let us start by recapping some recent changes in the cash management and payments system environment and analyzing those changes in light of the motivations of the major players, the corporations, the banks, and the Federal Reserve.

Technology

This has been the most constant and predictable trend—it keeps advancing. In both cash management and the payments system, available technology stays constantly ahead of the willingness to change to new methods. After all, systems are expensive and difficult to change, and a long time is required for a change as fundamental as electronic order processing and bill paying to be implemented throughout the economy. Technology also stays a step ahead of the law, as demononstrated by the Hutton incident, where new interpretations of check-kiting law had to be developed to apply to contemporary cash management methods and the unclear rights and liabilities of banks in the event of a payments-system-unwind scenario.

Financial Market Volatility

Varying rates of inflation in the United States and other countries, floating foreign exchange rates, and interest rate fluctuations are interrelated. They are fundamental elements of an international free market economy. They will remain a part of the economic environment in the absence of multigovernment regulatory measures.

Financial Product Innovation

The development or increased use of capital markets products, such as securitized assets, currency and interest rate swaps, long-dated forwards, interest rate caps and collars, debt defeasance, Euro commercial paper note issuance facilities, Eurobonds, ECU-denominated Eurobonds, and dual currency bonds are a reflection of the growing international scope of capital markets and a response to market volatility and bank disintermediation.

Increased Transaction Volume

Market volatility and new capital markets products have caused an increase in trading, primarily by financial institutions, and that has caused an increase in volume in the large dollar payments system.

Deregulation

Banks have been allowed to enter new areas of business, including some types of investment banking. They have also lost deposits to other financial institutions, such as money market funds and savings and loan associations, at just the time that financial market volatility and increased trading have increased banks' payments volume.

Consolidation

Corporations are consolidating their banking relationships, and the banks themselves are starting to merge. It is still to early to tell whether truly nationwide banking will develop, and if so, how long it will take.

Bank Risk

Corporations have become more concerned with the creditworthiness and capital adequacy of their banks for such reasons as recent bank failures caused by bad loans, increased off-balance-sheet liabilities, and increased payments systems risk.

Role of the Federal Reserve

The Fed has a complex role. It is the banking regulator, the holder of reserve accounts, the provider of payment settlement facilities, the lender of last resort, and the expander and contractor of the money supply.

Reactions

How have the major players reacted to these environmental changes? The reactions of the corporations, the banks, and the Federal Reserve can be analyzed in light of four basic motivations: generating income, reducing costs, reducing risks, and defining the ground rules. A summary of the motivations of each group follows.

Corporations

As technology made new cash management products available, corporations demanded them from their banks to improve their day-to-day control over working capital, to reduce their demand deposit levels, to increase their short-term investment earnings, and to make their treasury operations more cost-effective. As a result of the Hutton incident, lower interest rates, and a general concern with cost reduction and efficiency, corporate cash management priorities have begun to change. There is relatively less concern with float and more interest in the entire time line of cash management from booking the order to collecting cash. Corporations are aware of the long-term potential for cost reduction offered by electronic corporate trade payments and business data interchange, but they find established payment habits and quantifiable float benefits hard to give up. Both cost reduction and the perception of bank risk have motivated corporations to consolidate their banking relationships. The Hutton affair provided a catalyst for defining the ground rules and in some ways marked a maturing of the art of cash management. It provided a good excuse for corporations to review policies and procedures, internally and with their banks, vendors, and customers.

Banks

The development of cash management services was motivated by corporate demand and by the potential that noncredit services offered for revenue diversification and risk reduction. Deregulation, volatility in the financial markets, a changing role in the intermediation process, and competition with other types of financial institutions motivated banks to expand trading for their own account in government securities, foreign exchange, and interest rate futures and options. It also motivated them to expand products that created off-balance-sheet exposure, such as standby letters of credit, swaps, and note issuance facilities. Large money center banks started to move in the direction of investment banking, arranging loans for a fee, packaging them, selling them to investors, and thus keeping them off the balance sheet. The new financial instruments and increased trading caused increased money transfer volume. Increased transaction volume and off-balance-sheet risk, as well as loan losses in some sectors caused increased perception of bank risk. The voluntary rating and daylight overdraft cap program was an initiative by the banks in self-regulation, working in concert with the Federal Reserve. Defining, disclosing, and managing off-balance-sheet risks may provide the opportunity for a similar initiative.

Federal Reserve

Although it does not have the same profit motives as a private corporation or bank, the Fed is interested in minimizing the cost to the taxpayer of running the system. The Monetary Control Act helped the Fed with that objective by requiring it to charge for the services provided to banks and other financial institutions and mandated that the Fed reduce float in the system. As a result, the Fed became both a regulator and a competitor. To reduce risk, the Fed has worked with the banking industry on a program to reduce daylight overdrafts and has indicated that it may tighten further the caps as soon as the results of the current program have been evaluated. The Fed has also proposed risk-related capital guidelines applying to off-balance-sheet liabilities as well as the balance sheet accounts. The two other bank regulatory bodies, the Comptroller of the Currency and the Federal Deposit Insurance Corporation, have made similar proposals.

Questions and Issues

Corporate financial officers and bankers might keep the following unresolved questions and issues in mind as events in cash management and the payments system unfold in the next year or so.

Consolidation

How fast will interstate banking develop? Will increased consolidation of the banks result in a smaller number of stronger, better capitalized banks with less perceived risk? Will some big banks stretch their management and acquisition dollar resources too far in an effort to gain market share?

Bank Services

How will the trends of bank consolidation, fewer banks offering all services, more niche players, more nonbank providers of cash management services, and more hard-nosed pricing by the banks affect the choice, quality, and price of services offered to the corporation? Will the regionals gain increased market share in cash management services because of lower costs and the perception of better operating performance? How many of the money center banks will strike back by buying smaller banks and setting up de novo operations in other states?

Self Regulation

Will the voluntary rating program succeed as an experiment in self-regulation by the banking industry and set a precedent for years to come, or will self-rating by the banks at levels higher-than-justified be self-defeating?

Reevaluating of Each Payment Network's Function

Is further analysis of the payments system the task of the Fed, a banking industry committee, or both working together? Will money transfers be divided in two types, one having immediate time priority and the other required to reach its destination only by the end of the day? As new money transfer mechanisms are designed, can the requirements of the lower priority, same-day money transfers and the increased encryption and security features that some would like to see for ACH corporate trade payments all be wrapped into one system?

Objectives and Policies of the Fed

Will the Fed push money transfer volume into checks and ACH payments with the daylight overdraft limits program? In opposing large dollar payments over the ACH at the same time, will it be pushing in two opposite directions at once? What are the long-term ramifications of the Fed as both regulator and competitor of the banks?

Methods to Spread Payments System Risk

What new measures can be developed to spread the risk that exists on the CHIPS system today? Receiver guarantees, whereby the receiving bank assumes the credit risk of the sending bank and in turn provides finality of payment to its customer? A member indemnity program similar to those on the stock and commodity exchanges? Insurance? How could the risks be quantified for the purposes of insurance or indemnity?

New Payments System Conventions

How successful will the Fed funds netting program and the new timing conventions proposed by the American Bankers Association be in reducing daylight overdrafts? How long will it take for the banks to develop a mechanism for rolling over commercial paper? Will the Fed be successful in reducing daylight overdrafts? Will a book entry program be a solution? How rapidly will book entry systems develop in other securities markets? Will that help in the development of a worldwide securities market?

Appendix A
United States Code
Title 18
Crimes and Criminal Procedure
Chapter 63, Mail Fraud

Section 1341 – Frauds and Swindles

Whoever, having devised or intending to devise any scheme or artifice to defraud, or for obtaining money or property by means of false or fraudulent pretenses, representations, or promises, or to sell, dispose of, loan, exchange, alter, give away, distribute, supply, or furnish or procure for unlawful use any counterfeit or spurious coin, obligation, security, or other article, or anything represented to be or intimated or held out to be such counterfeit or spurious article, for the purpose of executing such scheme or artifice or attempting so to do, places in any post office or authorized depository for mail matter, any matter or thing whatever to be sent or delivered by the Postal Service, or takes or receives therefrom, any such matter or thing, or knowingly causes to be delivered by mail according to the direction thereon, or at the place at which it is directed to be delivered by the person to whom it is addressed, any such matter or thing, shall be fined not more than $1,000 or imprisoned not more than five years, or both.

Section 1343 – Fraud by Wire, Radio, or Television

Whoever, having devised or intending to devise any scheme or artifice to defraud, or for obtaining money or property by means of false or fraudulent pretenses, representations, or promises, transmits or causes to be transmitted by means of wire, radio, or television communication in interstate or foreign commerce, any writings, signs, signals, pictures, or sounds for the purpose of executing such scheme or artifice, shall be fined not more than $1,000 or imprisoned not more than five years, or both.

Section 1344 – Bank Fraud

(a) Whoever knowingly executes, or attempts to execute a scheme or artifice

(1) to defraud a federally chartered or insured financial institution; or

(2) to obtain any of the moneys, funds, credits, assets, securities or other property owned by or under the custody or control of a federally chartered or insured financial institution by means of false or fraudulent pretenses, representations, or promises, shall be fined not more than $10,000, or imprisoned not more than five years, or both.

(b) As used in this section, the term "federally chartered or insured financial institution" means

(1) a bank with deposits insured by the Federal Deposit Insurance Corporation;

(2) an institution with accounts insured by the Federal Savings and Loan Insurance Corporation;

(3) a credit union with accounts insured by the National Credit Union Administration Board;

(4) a Federal home loan bank or a member, as defined in section 2 of the Federal Home Loan Bank act (12 U.S.C. 1422), of the Federal home loan bank system; or

(5) a bank, banking association, land bank, intermediate credit bank, bank for cooperatives, production credit association, land bank association, mortgage association, trust company, savings bank, or other banking of financial institution organized or operating under the laws of the United States.

Section 1345 – Injunctions against Fraud

Whenever it shall appear that any person is engaged or is about to engage in any act which constitutes or will constitute a violation of this chapter, the Attorney General may initiate a civil proceeding in a district court of the United States to enjoin such violation. The court shall proceed as soon as practicable to the hearing and determination of such an action, as is warranted to prevent a continuing and substantial injury to the United States or to any person or class of persons for whose protection the action is brought. A proceeding under this section is governed by the Federal Rules of Civil Procedure, except that, if an indictment has been returned against the respondent, discovery is governed by the Federal Rules of Criminal Procedure.

Appendix B
Corporate Questionnaire Selected Responses

What cash management procedures does your corporation consider to be either unethical or subject to possible legal problems in the future? Check all that apply:

Any systems designed to extend disbursing float	21 %
Paying East Coast vendors from West Coast banks and/or mailing points and vice versa	32
Sending checks to a company's office rather than a designated lockbox	33
Rotating disbursement points to deoptimize vendors' lockbox configurations	39
Anticipatory drafting	33
Drawing on uncollected funds in banks that do not have sophisticated float-tracking system	70
Altering checks so that they cannot be processed by banks' high speed equipment	87
Drawing on uncollected funds when not covered by agreement with bank	63
Overdrafts at any time	30
Uncollected funds at any time	12

How has the relative importance of your cash management objectives changed during the last year? Check one for each item:

	More Important	Less Important	No Change
Minimize internal book balances	23 %	1 %	72 %
Minimize bank demand balances	43	2	55
Provide adequate compensation to banks	20	6	73
Maximize return on excess cash	38	4	57
Minimize collection float	39	1	59
Maximize disbursement float	14	10	73
Minimize bank fees and other external costs	59	3	37
Minimize internal cost of running cash management function	44	4	51
Use most efficient tools offered by leading cash management banks	47	1	49

In what ways is the cash management function measured quantitatively in your company? Check one for each item.

	Yes	No	Considering in Future
Profit center	5 %	82 %	5 %
Average level of cash versus target	60	29	5
Days sales outstanding	36	53	0
Accounts receivable turnover	33	53	1
Return on invested cash	52	32	5
Bank compensation versus target	55	32	6

What nonquantitative measures of the cash management function does your corporation have? Check all that apply:

Overall quality of bank relationships	86 %
Conformance with accepted practices	62
Use of state-of-the-art techniques	62
Quality of information to management	59
Quality of forecasts	59
Barometer of company liquidity	34

How have your criteria for evaluating principal banking relationships changed in the last year? Check one for each criterion:

	More Important	Less Important	No Change
Evaluation of management	24 %	1 %	72 %
Importance of bank in future	50	3	45
Credit extension	38	6	54
Investment banking capabilities	20	7	70
Quality and innovation of non-credit services	54	3	42
Pricing	55	2	41
Responsiveness	59	1	38
Bank capital adequacy and creditworthiness	55	2	41
Availability schedule	21	2	74
Correspondent bank network	7	9	81
Branch network—domestic	9	6	82
Branch network—international	18	6	74

Do you plan to collect some or all of your trade payments through the ACH or a similar electronic payment system? Check one:

Yes 52 % No 48 %

If the answer to the above is no, what is your reason? Check all that apply?

Believe payors will resist because of float loss	49 %
Believe payors will resist for administrative reasons	40
Will incur internal administrative resistance	18
Would not make the switch until ACH payments became industry practice	49
Not familiar with ACH and related bank services	5
Have doubts about Federal Reserve and commercial bank commitment to develop comprehensive electronic payment network	18

Do you plan to use the ACH or a similar electronic method for disbursements in the future? Check one:

Yes, for small dollar items (payments to individuals)	14 %
Yes, for large dollar items (trade payments)	12
Yes, for all items	12
No	27
Uncertain at this time	33

If the answer to the above is no, what is your reason? Check all that apply:

Do not want to give up collection float	59 %
Will incur internal administrative resistance	28
Expect customer resistance for administrative reasons despite float benefits	33

In what instruments do you invest your excess cash?

Commercial paper	63 %
Repos	63
Certificates of deposit	63
Euro time deposits	59
Bankers' acceptances	39
Euro CDs	35
Euro commercial paper	21
Interest bearing bank account	19
Money market fund	11
Master notes	10
Bank sweep account	9

If there were money transfer delays because of bank daylight overdraft limits, what kinds of your transactions do you think might be affected? Check all that apply:

Commercial paper issuance and investments	43
Payments within own corporate network	32
Payments to and from suppliers and customers	32
Other investment commitments	32
Government securities investments (secondary market)	20
Syndicate settlements	3

Have your banks discussed any of the measures listed below to deal with possible delays caused by daylight overdraft limits? Check all that apply:

Higher priced priority transfers	23
Charges for daylight overdrafts	23
Individual customer daylight overdraft limits	45

Appendix C
Bank Questionnaire Selected Responses

Which of the following cash management services do you offer? Check all that apply:

Computerized balance reporting	96%
Computerized transaction reporting	91
Computerized money transfer initiation	70
Real time (intraday) balance and transaction information	38
Lockboxes	
Wholesale	100
Retail	75
Controlled disbursement	85
Zero balance accounts	95
Payable through drafts	89
Depostitory transfer checks	
Telephone instructions to bank	89
Electronic initiation by customer	23
Clearing accounts	
Corporate	
Domestic	77
International	43
Bank	
Domestic	83
Indernational	49
Treasury workstations	47
Domestic consulting	43
International consulting	17
International balance reporting	36
International transaction reporting	
Amounts only	26
Full details	21
International collections through lockboxes and money transfer intercept points	9
International concentration accounts	11

How would you rate the following within your bank to the extent that they support your efforts to develop, manage, and sell noncredit services? Check one for each item:

	Good	Needs Improvement
Accuracy of unit costing	38 %	62 %
Accuracy of volume count	85	15
Competitive intelligence on pricing	55	45
Customer market research	48	52
Creativity in developing new products	69	31
Sales training for specialists	61	29
Sales training for relationship managers	44	56

How would you rate your own bank's ability to measure individual customer relationship profitability? Check one:

Very accurate	25 %
Somewhat accurate	60
Not very accurate	15

Which of the following statements describe your bank's policies toward overdrafts? Check all that apply:

Occasional ledger overdrafts and uncollected funds are tolerated, provided that average collected balances are at an agreed-on level, and overdrafts charges are paid and balances maintained according to agreement.	70 %
Occasional uncollected funds are tolerated provided that average collected balances are maintained at an agreed upon level.	51
Overdrafts of any kind are against bank policy	42
Our bank is more tolerant of overdrafts among large correspondent bank and corporate "clearing" customers	8
There is no policy; we deal with overdrafts on a case-by-case basis	6

What short term investment alternatives for overnight and longer periods do you offer your corporate customers? Check all that apply:

Overnight repos	75 %
Commercial paper	74
Bankers' acceptances	66
Euro time deposits	55
Sweep account—defined rate	45
Master notes	45
Euro CDs	43
Euro commercial paper	23
Sweep account—defined spread below LIBOR or other index	9

Are you considering any of the measures listed below to deal with daylight overdraft limits either this year or in the future should caps be tightened? Check all that apply:

Individual-customer daylight overdrafts limits	87 %
Netting Fed funds rollovers	42
Borrowing Fed funds for more than one day	42
Charging customers for daylight overdrafts	38
Prioritizing transfers by customer	34
First come, first served for fully funded customers	34
Higher prices for priority money transfers	24
Variable rate for overnight Fed funds depending on when borrower agrees to return them	19

What kinds of transactions do you think would be most affected if daylight overdraft caps were further tightenend? Check all that apply:

Commercial paper issuance and investments	42
Government securities investments (secondary market)	42
Other investment commitments	42
Payments to and from suppliers and customers	21
Payments within customer corporate networks	24
Syndicate settlements	15

Appendix D
Contributors

The following individuals, a number of whom are quoted in the book, provided invaluable information and insights in the form of both interviews and written material:

Donald Anderson
Manager-Accounting Department
Federal Reserve Bank of New York

Paul Beehler
Senior Vice President
E. F. Hutton

Dean A. Bitner
Director of EFT Development
Corporate Treasurer's Office
Sears, Roebuck and Co.

T. J. Britt
Manager-Cash Management
IBM Corp.

Joanne F. Burns
Vice President
Bank of Boston

Marshall T. Butler
Manager-Global Liquidity
Administration
Combustion Engineering, Inc.

Neil Byl
Manager-Passenger Sales Accounting
United Airlines

Anthony J. Carfang
Principal
Treasury Strategies, Inc.

David C. Cates
President
Cates Consulting Analysts, Inc.

Thomas A. Ciconte
Manager-Banking
Hercules Inc.

Peter B. Clark
Trial Attorney
U.S. Department of Justice

K. C. (Charlie) Clayton
Manager-Banking &
Cash Management
Shell Oil Co.

John F. Lee
Executive Vice President
New York Clearing House Assoc.

H. "Buddy" Le Tourneau
Senior Vice President
NCNB Nat'l. Bank of North Carolina

Larry Marks
President
Phoenix-Hecht, Inc.

Leslie N. Masonson
Vice President
Citibank

Jack M. Meckler
Senior Vice President
First Wachovia Corporate Services

Ray M. McClintock
Vice President
Mellon Bank

James J. McDermott, Jr.
Senior VP & Director of Research
Keefe, Bruyette & Woods, Inc.

David L. McKinney
Cash Management
IBM Corp.

James E. Nave
Vice President-Cash Mgmt. Group
First City Nat'l. Bank of Houston

Cassa Coulter Palmer
Vice President
Philadelphia National Bank

Francis P. Polney
Assistant Treasurer
International Paper Co.

Anthony F. Rash
Senior Financial Analyst
Hercules Inc.

Lee Epstein
Vice President/Financial Consultant
Shearson Lehman Brothers, Inc.

Edward C. Ettin
Deputy Director
Division of Research & Statistics
Board of Governors-Federal Reserve System

Robert P. Ford
Vice President
Citibank

Robert L. Foster
Manager-Banking Services
3M Corporation

David D. Fox
Executive Vice President
Greenwich Research Associates

Robert Gant
Vice President
NCNB National Bank of North Carolina

Joseph A. Glade
Division Manager-Cash Management
AT&T

D. Huckins
Manager-Cash Management
United Airlines

Charlene Karsner
President
KCP Ltd.

Nelson Kibler
Partner
Touche Ross & Co.

Jim R. Kirkendoll
Manager-Cash Management & Banking
E.I. duPont deNemours & Co., Inc.

Scott E. Knudson
Analyst
Board of Governors of the Federal Reserve System

Gregory P. Kurts
Associate Treasury Analyst
Alexander & Alexander, Inc.

Robert W. Quinlan
Vice President
Equitable Bank, Baltimor

Neill Reilly
Managing Director
Bank Valuation

William W. Renshaw
Partner
Arthur Young & Co.

Seymour Rosen
Vice President
Citibank

Lawrence C. Russell
Executive Vice President
First National Bank of Chicago

Patricia M. Russell
Assistant Vice President
MBank Houston

Jack Shaw
President
Electronic Cash Management, Inc.

Virginia E. Sloan
Assistant Counsel
House of Representatives
Subcommittee on Crime
Committee on the Judiciary

Fred W. Stuckwisch
Consultant
U.S. General Accounting Office

Randall P. Symes
Manager-Banking Section
E.I. duPont deNemours & Co., Inc.

Eric A. Thomson
President
Valutech

Thomas C. Tucker
Director-Corporate Service Group
Bank Administration Institute

John Yaecker
Manager-Banking
J. C. Penney Co., Inc.

Benson K. Woo
Director-Worldwide Banking & U.S. Cash Management
General Motors Corp.